Vacuum Kiln Drying for Woodworkers

How to Build and Use a Vacuum Kiln for Drying Wood

Joshua Salesin

Vacuum Kiln Drying for Woodworkers – How to Build and Use a Vacuum Kiln for Drying Wood, by Joshua Salesin

Published by:
Salesin Enterprises
P. O. Box 701
Santa Cruz, CA 95061
info@vacuumkilndrying.com
www.vacuumkilndrying.com

1ˢᵗ edition: May 2008.
2ⁿᵈ edition: May 2010.
3ʳᵈ edition: May 2014.
4ᵗʰ edition: May 2017.

ISBN-10: 1546686126
ISBN-13: 978-1546686125

Printed in the U.S.A.

Contents

Preface to the 4th Edition _____ 6

Foreword_____ 9

Acknowledgments_____ 11

Disclaimer & Agreement _____ 12

Introduction _____ 13

Section 1: The Nature of Wood

    Why dry wood at all? _____ 15

    The nature of "green" wood _____ 18

    The nature of water in wood _____ 19

        What is free water? _____ 19

        What is bound water? _____ 20

        What is fiber saturation point? _____ 20

        Why does it matter? _____ 20

    Why does wood crack?_____ 20

    What is dry? _____ 22

    How dry is dry enough? _____ 23

    Methods to speed up drying time _____ 25

Section 2: How & Why Vacuum Kiln Drying Works

    Why vacuum dry? _____ 27

    Why does vacuum drying work? _____ 30

    How does a vacuum kiln work? _____ 33

    Methods to heat wood in a vacuum_____ 34

Section 3: How to Build a Vacuum Kiln

Details of required items

Vacuum pump _____ 39

Vacuum chamber _____ 46

End plates _____ 48

Valves & gauge _____ 50

Heater _____ 54

    Convection 55

    Radiation 56

    Conduction 56

Temperature controller _____ 61

Temperature sensor _____ 62

Electrical socket _____ 65

Shelf _____ 65

Moisture meter _____ 65

Details of optional items

Fan _____ 67

Moisture trap _____ 68

Drain _____ 70

Clamps _____ 72

Programmable timer _____ 72

Solenoid valve _____ 72

Assembly and troubleshooting

Assembly and troubleshooting _____ 74

Cost to build

Cost to build _____ 76

Section 4: Additional Vacuum Kiln Examples

Pre-made vacuum kilns _____ 77

Adaptations from readers _____ 81

Section 5: Process for Vacuum Drying Wood

The procedure in detail _____ 91

Examples for heating various loads _____ 94

Appendix I – Drying Template _____ 103

Appendix II – Wiring Diagrams for the
        Temperature Controller _____ 107

Appendix III – Modifications for
        Stabilizing Wood_____ 111

Appendix IV – Reference Charts _____ 113

   Boiling point of water _____ 113

   Vacuum attainable at altitude _____ 116

   Equilibrium moisture content_____ 113

   Comparison of pressure measurements_____ 117

   Conversion factors _____ 118

Appendix V – Online Resources _____ 119

About the Author _____ 120

Preface to the 4th Edition

More than ten years ago, I was inspired to share how to build and use a vacuum kiln for drying wood. I knew other woodworkers would enjoy the benefits of drying wood faster and more reliably by using this fairly simple apparatus. I figured I could keep things short and to the point, that people would read it cover to cover, build their kiln, dry some wood and get on with making their project.

Without a scientific background or any experience using lab equipment, I didn't fully appreciate the intricacies and variables of vacuum kiln drying. Of course, I needed to describe what parts to buy and how to put it together, as well as explain how to use it. But I also thought it would also be helpful to explain about wood in general and why it naturally cracks as it dries. It also seemed important to provide an understanding of how and why vacuum systems work better than other methods of drying wood. To do that, more "scientific" details, such as how the boiling point of water varies with vapor pressure, how moisture is accurately measured and how different environments impact the drying process were included to help everyone successfully use the vacuum kiln. In so doing, the first edition grew from what might have been a pamphlet into a booklet.

The second edition added further details to address the most common questions, including alternate methods of heating wood, examples of small ready-made vacuum chambers for those who didn't want to build their own kiln but still wanted to take advantage of the benefits of vacuum kiln drying, along with updated resources and parts suppliers.

For the third edition, I expanded the sections pertaining to the three most important elements: vacuum pumps, heating the lumber and measuring moisture. I added callout boxes with in-depth answers to common questions and placed these throughout the text where topics were initially explained rather than compiled in a separate FAQ section as done previously.

In this fourth edition, I present a stronger bias toward building a conduction based system including a revamp of my original design along with new photos and building instructions. There is also a new section that presents a variety of vacuum chambers, with photos and details of commercially available kilns as well as examples from readers who created their own variations of the design presented in this book. The section that details the technique of vacuum drying is also expanded with new photos and explanations for how to arrange and heat various types of kiln loads for particular kinds of lumber.

As the number of ways to customize a vacuum kiln drying setup has grown, so too has the potential expense. While the cost for a used vacuum pump has remained consistent throughout the years, the basic hardware store parts used to build the kiln have steadily increased. Therefore, I have added a list of "project parts" to the Online Resource page where you can link to the latest pricing, compare similar products, read reviews and learn more about the items needed to make your kiln. This page also includes other pertinent links to articles related to wood drying and vacuum technology, downloads to useful templates and reference charts and other items you may find worthwhile. An overview of these topics can be found in Appendix V along with the web page address.

As you learn about vacuum kiln drying, develop plans to build your kiln and dry all types of wood, keep in mind there are different ways to achieve the same result. This book provides one approach while detailing several variations. Each version I've seen built (all from people who started by reading this book) is unique and often improves on one aspect or another to address a particular need.

I am always grateful when readers share examples and stories of how they were inspired by the ideas in this book, then built their own vacuum kiln to dry wood and are now making beautiful and useful things. Please keep sending your success stories as well as your questions—it inspires me to continue learning more about this method and to share that information with everyone in the next edition.

I am truly excited to see this previously unused system for small-scale wood drying develop a community of enthusiasts!

Joshua Salesin
May 2017

Foreword

This book was written to share information about a method for drying wood that is not well known among woodworking hobbyists. The technique I describe can be used for rough-turned work as well as milled lumber, limited only by the size of the chamber. All types of woodworking benefit from properly seasoned wood and the method I describe for achieving this is quick and easy.

In the fall of each year, I show my woodwork to the public as part of my community's open studio art tour. A few years ago, a well-known woodturner, Mike Shuler, stopped by for a visit. As we discussed some of my turned boxes (pictured below) I explained that even though quite a bit of work went into making them— hand-chased threaded lids, inset tops, and a rose engine cut interior—probably the most difficult part was figuring out if the wood was truly dry. If not, the top would no longer fit perfectly with the base after the pieces changed to a new "dry" state.

It was that unseen but most important factor that ultimately determined the success of the box and all the work that went into its creation. After hearing my predicament, Mike invited me to see the vacuum kiln he invented for drying wood. Of course, I took him up on the offer!

Now, after having built my own vacuum kiln, it has become the preferred method of drying wood for all my projects. Over the years, I have successfully dried wood for hundreds of turnings. I hope this book will help you find the perfect drying method for all your wood projects too!

Acknowledgments

Without the generous time, information, and inspiration given to me by Mike Shuler, my vacuum kiln would never have been built and this book would not have been written. In addition, the kind folks at Provac in Santa Cruz, CA provided parts at friendly prices along with valuable expertise.

Much of the material contained in this book was first organized as a presentation to woodturning and ornamental turning clubs. Special thanks go to those audience members who offered their feedback to help improve this resource.

Since publishing the first edition nearly ten years ago, I have been contacted by many people who are excited to share the results of their vacuum kiln drying setup along with photos and details of improvements they made. Some of these are featured in the pages of this book and I am grateful for their permission to do so and for the effort made to share all the specifics. In particular, thanks to Al Collins, Fred Connell, Jeff Hankinson, Brian Jackson, and Charles Waggoner.

Disclaimer & Agreement

This book is designed to provide information about building and using a homemade vacuum kiln for drying wood. There may be some risk involved with the application of information contained in this book. Its contents are to be considered non-expert opinion only and offered without warranty. You are solely responsible for your access to, use of and reliance on any content. You agree to conduct any necessary, appropriate, prudent, or judicious investigation, inquiry, research, and due diligence with respect to the safe and appropriate use of its contents. The author and publisher shall not assume any responsibility for any incident, accident, or otherwise regarding the use of information contained in this document. No warranty or representation, either expressed or implied, is made with respect to the quality, accuracy, safety or fitness of any part of this document. The author and publisher shall have neither liability nor responsibility to any person or entity with respect to any loss, damage, adverse effects, or any other consequences caused, or alleged to have been caused, directly or indirectly, from the use of information, advise, suggestions, procedures, or instructions given in this publication. Please do not implement the actions suggested in this publication if you are unwilling to assume any and all risk.

Mention or display of a trademark, proprietary product or firm in text or figures does not constitute an endorsement and does not imply approval to the exclusion of other suitable products or firms.

Introduction

This book was written to help you learn how to assemble and use a homemade vacuum kiln for quickly drying small batches of wood. It presents a cost-effective solution for an independent woodworker or hobbyist based on the same techniques used in larger and significantly more expensive commercial vacuum drying systems.

First, I explain a bit about the nature of wood followed by an overview of how and why vacuum kiln drying works. Next, I present all the details for how to build a wood drying vacuum kiln. Then, I show some variations that could be made including a few shortcuts. Finally, I cover the technique for quickly drying wood with the vacuum kiln so you can:

- make your projects *faster*. You'll no longer wait for months "watching wood dry" before you can use it.

- make your projects *better*. The items you create won't unexpectedly warp or crack and won't have stains or spots coloring the wood. The result: boxes with lids that keep a perfect fit, marquetry and joinery that remains perfectly flat and projects that stay glued tight.

Meet the author's vacuum kiln

My first vacuum kiln was constructed from many used and discarded materials—a large PVC pipe, Corian off-cuts, previously used tubing, an extra closet shelf and an old vacuum pump. After adding a few new parts from the hardware store and other items purchased online, the vacuum kiln was born! The photo below shows the result:

It was a fairly straightforward project and the benefits of its application became immediately obvious—the time to dry wood was drastically reduced! What used to take months or years now takes a few days or hours. The process completely changed how I work.

Section 1: The Nature of Wood

Why dry wood at all?

- More stable material
  - Less likely to crack
  - Less likely to warp
- Higher quality material
  - Less likely to discolor or decay
  - Less susceptible to insect damage
- More design choices
- Quicker path from inspiration to creation
- Save inventory space
- Prevent SawStop® false triggers

Air-drying a slab-cut log. The lumber industry produces more than 30 billion board feet per year in the USA alone.

While some woodworkers use wet wood for carving or "green turning" to good effect, most of the time wood is more usable when it is dry because it is stable—it will keep its shape, quality, and color (more or less) after you finish making your piece. And since wet lumber requires a uniform thickness to prevent cracking, it further limits the types of pieces you can make. Simply put, dry wood allows for more design choices.

When you have dry wood on hand, you can try out new ideas more quickly. A shorter time from inspiration to creation can

This oak bowl was made from fresh-cut wood and turned perfectly round. It warped and cracked as it dried to its current shape. Surprise!

really speed up the process of developing a new line of work and getting it out to a gallery, craft show or collector. And a faster production cycle means much less wood in inventory, which yields more of that valuable shop space.

There is an additional benefit especially for owners of SawStop® saws. Using a SawStop® to cut wood that *seems* dry on the outside but actually has high moisture content inside could cause the safety system to engage, destroying the expensive single-use brake cartridge and blade in the process. Using vacuum kiln dried wood, you can be assured that the moisture content is consistent throughout each piece of wood. In fact, equalizing the moisture content from the core to the surface of wood is unique to the physics of drying wood with a vacuum kiln (and is further explained in Section 2).

Common Question: SawStop®

"I use a SawStop® saw. How can I be sure the wood I dry will not have moisture in the middle and cause the safety system to engage?"

Even though a two-pin moisture meter cannot accurately read moisture content of wood fibers deeper than a quarter inch, the physics of drying wood in a vacuum kiln causes an equalizing of moisture from the core to the surface of wood. Therefore, a moisture reading at the outside will be very similar to the inside. If you have material you suspect might trigger the SawStop® brake, you can make a cut with the saw in bypass mode and it will signal if it would have set off the brake. Then, you can quantify this using your moisture meter and keep a record for that species for future reference.

The nature of "green" wood

I've turned a bunch of fresh-cut "green" wood on the lathe—some of it with good results. But it can be unpredictable for a couple of reasons:

- Trees grow with internal stress
- Trees contain a large amount of water

Trees grow with all kinds of internal stress and when brought down begin to release that stress. This results in all types of warping.

Trees also contain a tremendous amount of water that must leave the wood as it reaches equilibrium with the surrounding environment. Water often constitutes more weight than the actual wood, so the

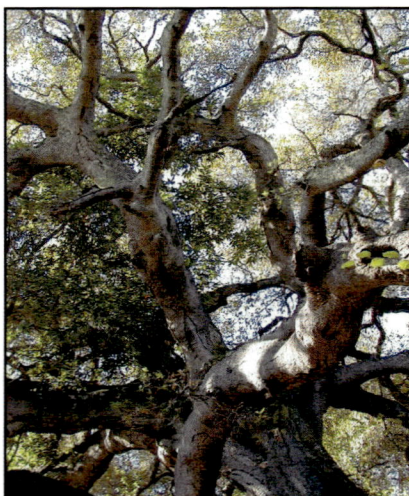

Many trees naturally grow with lots of internal stress. Others are stressed by their environment.

shrinkage that occurs with the drying process results in significant physical changes that, if not controlled in some way, almost always results in cracking.

The shrinkage that occurs transpires in three different directions simultaneously: radial, longitudinal, and tangential. The shrinkage is not equal in all directions and is different for each wood species, with some types shrinking six times more than others in any particular direction. Also, in the case of both cracking and warping, some species are significantly more stable than others.

Wood expands and contracts different amounts depending on the grain.

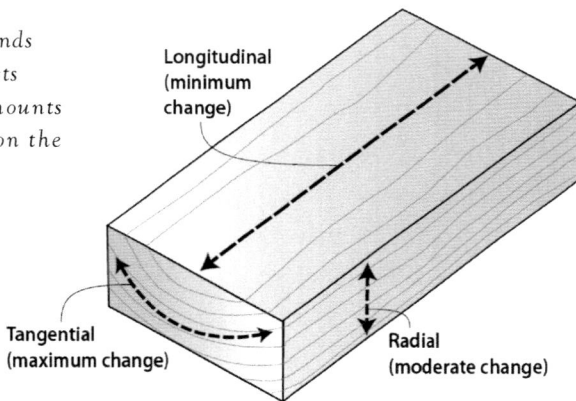

Longitudinal (minimum change)

Tangential (maximum change)

Radial (moderate change)

The nature of water in wood

What is free water?

The bulk of water contained in the cell cavities of wood is only held by capillary forces. It is not bound chemically and it is called "free water." When fresh-cut wood begins to dry, the first water to evaporate is the free water. However, most physical properties such as strength and shrinkage are unaffected by the removal of free water.

What is bound water?

Sometimes called hygroscopic water, "bound water" is attached to the wood cell walls by hydrogen bonds. The cells readily exchange moisture with the ambient air until they reach a moisture content that is in balance with the surrounding environment. This requires most bound water to leave the wood.

What is fiber saturation point?

As wood dries, the free water in the cell cavities is drawn away first. Once the free water evaporates or is removed through a drying technique, the bound water from the cell walls is gradually released. The fiber saturation point (FSP) is the stage of drying where free water is completely gone from the wood cell cavities, and the cell walls are still completely saturated with bound water. For most wood, the fiber saturation point is about 25% to 30% moisture content.

Why does it matter?

Here's the important part: if the moisture content (MC) in the wood is above the fiber saturation point, the physical properties of the wood will not change. If MC is below FSP, then the wood begins to undergo physical changes.

Why does wood crack?

Wood splits through a two-step process:
1. Adjacent layers with different FSP cause stress
2. When stress exceeds strength, splitting occurs

Wood dries from every grain direction somewhat, but primarily through the end grain. This naturally results in the outer layers and ends to dry out more quickly and completely than the interior. When these outer layers dry below the fiber saturation point while the interior remains above the FSP, drying stresses occur between the various wood tissue layers. When the *stress* across the layers exceeds the *strength* across the layers, splits and cracks occur.

Therefore, to successfully control defects in the drying process, a balance between the rate of evaporation of moisture from the surface and the rate of outward movement of moisture from the interior of the wood must be maintained.

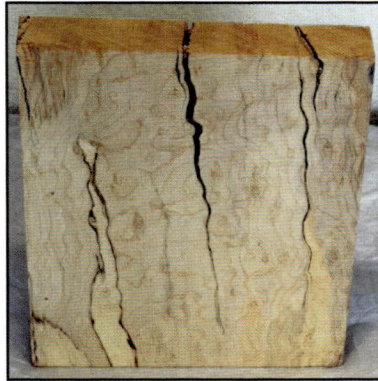

This spalted maple block split because the stress caused by drying was greater than its strength.

When air-drying wood, this is often mitigated by cutting a tree into boards of equal thickness or turning a log down to a uniformly thick bowl, both of which reduce the chance of splitting as the wood dries. The distinct advantages of drying wood in a vacuum chamber compared to this air-drying method are detailed in Section 2.

What is dry?

- Wood is never completely "dry"
- Moisture content of "dry" wood varies with relative humidity and temperature

Wood is never completely "dry"—there is no one final dimension of a piece of wood. It will continue to shrink and swell as it exchanges moisture with the environment. The term moisture content is used to express the range between a material's saturation point—100% of the water it can hold—and the opposite that contains no water at all (0% MC). When the moisture content is in balance with the relative humidity at a specific temperature, it is called the equilibrium moisture content (EMC) of the wood.

The EMC varies with the climate of your geographic location, the changing seasons, and also the day-to-day weather. Where I live, the relative humidity fluctuates daily as the fog rolls in off the ocean, and storms can also bring drastic changes.

The Equilibrium Moisture Content chart in Appendix IV shows that the EMC of wood changes quite a lot with the ambient relative humidity and to a lesser degree with temperature. You can see that "dry" varies from 4% to 24% depending on your climate!

Common Question: Shrinking

"Does wood shrink more using vacuum kiln drying compared with air drying?"

Wood will shrink to the same shape and size when dried to the same moisture content (MC) regardless of drying method used (but it might not crack using one drying method versus another). Since the vacuum kiln allows wood to be dried to levels below equilibrium moisture content (EMC), it is possible to have more shrinkage when using a vacuum kiln. However, as the wood stabilizes to the relative humidity and temperature of the ambient air, it will end up the same shape and size as any other drying method that results in the same MC.

How dry is dry enough?

- Know the MC of your wood
- Match MC with projected EMC

Depending where and when you acquire your wood, it may need to be further "seasoned" in order to stabilize it before use. Wood that is sold commercially at the lumber store is usually dried to around 12% MC and further air-dries with time, eventually reaching equilibrium with the surrounding environment. Likewise, wood for use indoors, such as furniture, must be in equilibrium with the indoor climate to prevent unwanted changes.

When I send an item to a gallery or home in a different region, there is a good chance their environment will be different than mine. A different temperature and relative humidity will force the piece to lose or gain moisture, causing it to change shape. If the change happens very quickly, causing stress between various layers in the wood, it may even crack.

What to do? Your wood should be dried to the average equilibrium moisture content (EMC) of the environment where it will be placed into service. This will minimize any movement that might occur. Use the Equilibrium Moisture Content table in Appendix IV to find an appropriate target moisture level based on temperature and humidity.

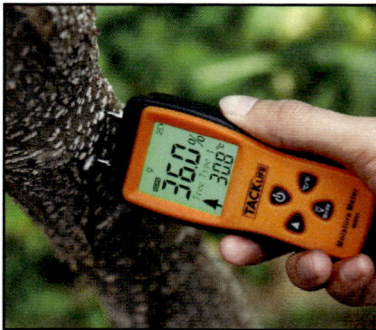

A two-prong moisture meter uses electrical resistance to instantly indicate the percentage of moisture in the wood. Photo courtesy of Tacklife.

To know if your wood is ready to use, you must know its moisture content. The first time I borrowed a moisture meter was an eye-opening experience. As I tested the various pieces of wood lying around, I immediately learned which ones were ready to use and which needed further drying. This was something I previously had no reliable way of knowing.

When creating precision fit pieces, such as boxes with lids, inlays, or laminate work, each of the parts will need to have the same moisture content. I aim for 7% to 8% MC since this is the level that wood stabilizes to in a climate-controlled room.

This might not be possible given the ambient conditions where you store your wood. Not possible, that is, without introducing artificial means to dry the wood! (Did I hear someone say, "vacuum kiln?")

Methods to speed up drying time

Wood will naturally dry as it is exposed to ambient air at the rate of about 1" thickness per year. However, this factor compounds as the wood increases in thickness, so a 5" thick piece of wood actually takes longer than five years to dry. In fact, it might take ten years depending on the type of wood, orientation of the grain, and drying conditions.

There are various methods to speed up the drying process:

- Air-dry, with the addition of:
    - "roughing out" the piece to remove as much unneeded material as possible
    - fan or convection container to create more air-flow across the wood surface
    - dehumidification system

- Heat, such as:
    - light bulb
    - electric pad
    - microwave
    - traditional oven
    - steam oven
    - boiling water
    - solar kiln
- Cold, such as:
    - freezing
    - refrigeration
- Displacement through soaking, such as:
    - alcohol
    - soap solution
    - salt or other chemical solutions
- Vacuum kiln

Each of these methods has a distinct set of requirements for success. I have tried them all, short of building a solar kiln or using chemical solutions, and found several clear advantages to vacuum kiln drying. These are discussed in the next section.

Vacuum kiln drying is one method used by the lumber industry. The photo shows the loading of a Vacu-Kiln 2000 system. Photo courtesy of Wood-Mizer Products, Inc.

Section 2: How and Why Vacuum Kiln Drying Works

Why vacuum dry?

Advantages
- Quickest method
- Highest quality lumber
- Uniform MC
- Can reduce MC ≤ EMC
- Saves space
- Less cumbersome

Disadvantages
- Kiln takes space
- Pump maintenance
- Pump noise & exhaust
- Expense

Let's look at the advantages in detail:

Vacuum kiln drying for wood is the quickest drying method. A load containing many pieces can generally be dried in one to three days, depending on the beginning moisture content. This is five to twelve times faster than conventional kilns and with higher quality results.

Vacuum kiln drying produces the highest quality lumber of all the drying methods because it greatly reduces drying defects, such as checking, cracking, twisting, bending and cupping. The wood is much less susceptible to fungal, mold or other discolorations. It doesn't endure the oxidation that occurs during prolonged air-drying so the result produces brighter and more saturated color. And since stickers are not needed for drying there are no sticker stains from uneven oxidation.

Vacuum kiln drying results in uniform moisture throughout the thickness of each piece. It does not over dry at the core or the outer layers. It also enables control over the final moisture content in ways that few other methods allow—wood can be dried to any MC regardless of environmental conditions.

Vacuum kiln drying can also save valuable shop space because the shorter turnaround time between acquiring and using the wood means less material in inventory and for a shorter period of time. The space that would have been used to store the wood while it air-dried can instead be used for other purposes.

The process involved in vacuum kiln drying is generally less cumbersome than most other methods. (The exact method I use is described in Section 5.) It is also worth noting that vacuum kiln drying uses less energy than conventional drying kilns.

Now let's look at the disadvantages:

While the overall setup is compact, some space is needed for the kiln and vacuum pump. (The setup shown in Section 3 fits on a 4' x 1½' shelf.) Maintenance of the vacuum pump such as oil changes, while easy, are required on a regular basis. The air quality and noise level around the vacuum pump will depend on the vacuum pump you use, but may be unpleasant. A commercially made vacuum kiln setup is also typically *very* expensive, but you're about to learn how to create a fully functional system for a few hundred dollars or less.

Common Question: Vacuum Drying 1

"This vacuum drying sounds like the answer to all my problems and opens up a whole new world of possibilities. Is it really as good as you say?"

I do believe vacuum kiln drying is your best bet. That's why I wanted to share the news and write this book! But there are other factors that can play a factor in whether wood cracks while drying; the more uniform the thickness and the more consistent the grain orientation, the better your results will be. You will not get 100% perfect results. No one does, not even professionals with $100,000 vacuum drying systems. Still, I don't think there is a better method for drying wood.

"How feasible is it to dry thick planks, perhaps 6/4, 8/4 or 12/4 that are 24" wide and up to 8' long?"

The setup described here can be scaled up to dry any dimension of lumber. Your challenges will be:

1. building a large and strong chamber that doesn't leak and can hold vacuum above 27 inHg.
2. slowly and uniformly heating all the lumber.
3. keeping moisture out of your vacuum pump using a trap and releasing potentially large amounts of water from the chamber using a drain system.

Each of the above items increase the cost from what is detailed in this book. You can learn more about commercial vacuum drying from related links in the Online Resources page (see Appendix V).

Common Question: Vacuum Drying 2

"I was hoping to build a vacuum kiln to dry green oak, down to about 20% MC for a traditional exposed panel infill frame. Will vacuum kiln drying work?"

If you're only going down to 20% MC your biggest challenge will be stopping the process before it gets too dry. The drying in this system is so rapid that when you achieve the proper temperature/vacuum combination, drying can quickly be reduced below 20% MC. Depending on your initial MC, you may need to slow down the drying process by adding steam to the chamber or wax to the end grain of your lumber. I'm sure it will be possible to achieve the desired MC with experimentation.

"Can I use vacuum drying for burl wood?"

Yes, vacuum drying works for any type of wood. Each type will dry differently depending on grain structure, density, moisture content and other particulars. I find burl is easier to dry (i.e.: dries quickly and without defects) because the grain structure is very consistent compared to other parts of the tree. Where you might need to pay more attention is when drying burl caps because the edges will be thinner than the middle. It is better (though not required) to have equal thickness for defect-free drying, the details of which are covered in Section 3 and 5. Always do some trial runs with smaller pieces. If the vacuum kiln is setup properly you will find a drying approach that works.

Why does vacuum drying work?

- Pressure gradient moves water toward surface

- Vacuum increases vapor pressure that converts water from liquid to gas

- Low heat = less defects, as wood is stronger

- Low heat + low oxygen = less fungus staining

- Vacuum + heat = exterminated insects

One reason for faster drying in a vacuum kiln system is that a pressure gradient is created between the core and the outside of a piece of wood. This pressure gradient is very effective in moving moisture, especially *free water*, from the core to the surface.

Another reason for faster drying is the increase in vapor pressure that results from drawing a vacuum. This causes water to change from a liquid to a gas at a lower temperature than normal. This increased vapor pressure is very effective in moving *bound water* from the wood cells.

By controlling temperature with a heater and vapor pressure with a vacuum pump, you can effectively control the boiling point of liquids—the state at which water vaporizes to a gas and rushes out of the wood.

This relationship of temperature and vapor pressure to the boiling point of water is shown in the graph below. (Vapor pressure can be measured in inches Hg VAC and is used throughout this book, often abbreviated as inHg.)

ºF

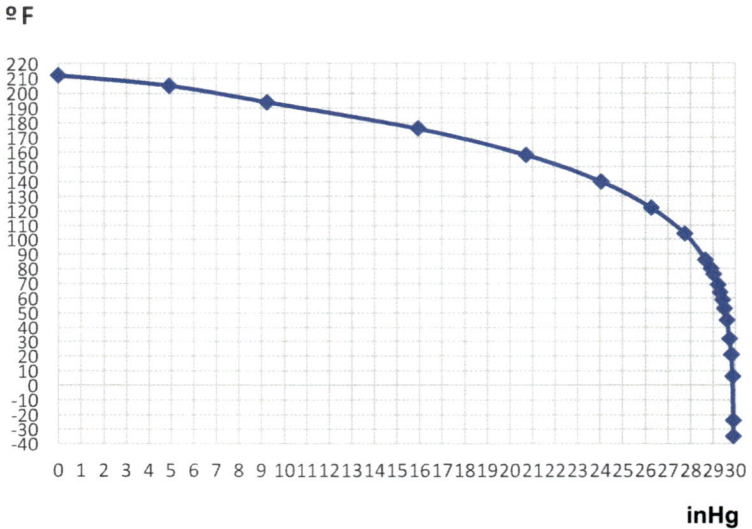

inHg

At sea level, water at a typical indoor temperature of 72ºF (22.2ºC) will boil in a vacuum at 29.12 inHg. By raising the temperature, the requirement to achieve such a strong vacuum is reduced. For example, at a temperature of 104ºF (40ºC) only 27.75 inHg is needed to cause water in the wood to vaporize.

Other factors such as altitude, the type of lumber and the way it is heated can affect the exact temperature required. However, the range between 100ºF (38ºC) and 120ºF (49ºC) works for most vacuum kiln drying situations. These relatively low temperatures are preferable to other methods of heating wood for drying because wood is stronger at a lower temperature and can withstand greater internal stress, resulting in fewer defects. In addition to the low operating temperature, the lack of oxygen inside a vacuum chamber results in considerably less potential for fungus to grow or wood stains to occur.

Another benefit of vacuum is that it can remove water from the bodies of insects. The food packing industry uses vacuum technology to kill insects before shipping some products, presumably without heat. A vacuum process that uses heat will further improve results. But thicker lumber and higher moisture content will require longer exposure time, with both higher vacuum and heat being preferable. While no official standard exists yet to ensure all bugs and larvae are exterminated, I have never had an insect problem with vacuum kiln dried lumber.

How does a vacuum kiln work?

1. Kiln is loaded with wood

2. Heat raises temperature of moisture inside wood

3. Vacuum is drawn on the chamber

4. Moisture vapor escapes from wood

5. Drying occurs quickly over a few days depending on beginning MC and wood species

Methods to heat wood in a vacuum

All vacuum kiln wood drying systems operate at sub-atmospheric pressure. The level of vacuum varies with the specific system, generally in the range of 27 to 29.9 inHg. The main difference between systems is the way they heat the lumber.

There are four methods to heat wood in a vacuum:

1. Discontinuous heat / vacuum
   - Alternates between operating at atmospheric pressure and under vacuum
   - Wood is heated when air is present
   - Residual heat in wood causes drying when combined with vacuum
   - Temperature and vacuum are regulated to control drying rate

2. Superheated steam
   - Alternates between operating at atmospheric pressure and under vacuum
   - Water vapor is used to transfer heat from coils to lumber
   - Water vapor is circulated by internal fans through lumber piled on stickers to create uniform humidity
   - Temperature, vacuum and humidity are each regulated to control drying rate

3. Radio frequency (RF)

- Vacuum is maintained continuously

- Electrodes are placed in and around the load to create a RF field that heats the lumber

- RF and vacuum are regulated to control drying rate

4. Platen / Direct contact

- Vacuum is maintained continuously

- Heated platens are placed in direct contact with the lumber

- Platens are heated by a thermal fluid (such as hot water) or by embedded electrical heaters

- Temperature and vacuum are regulated to control drying rate

A discontinuous vacuum drying system is the least expensive and quickest method to setup but it can be more challenging to operate because of the need to juggle between the vacuum and heating requirements. Details on this type of setup are covered in Section 4 and 5.

A superheated steam vacuum drying system is a variation of the discontinuous method described above. This allows evaporated steam to remain in (or be added to) the chamber which can prevent the lumber from over-drying or help condition lumber that is exceptionally prone to cracking. This method is not specifically detailed in this book other than describing the conditions that create moisture vapor and the procedure for retaining or releasing it.

Radio frequency (RF) vacuum drying uses radio waves to heat the lumber in the chamber and does so more quickly and evenly than other methods. It will also kill any insects in the wood. RF is used in various drying, disinfecting and food curing industries. This method is not specifically detailed in this book as it requires electrode heat and RF resistive chamber materials that I have not researched or tested. However, all the concepts and techniques presented here still apply.

Direct contact systems utilize heating elements layered between the lumber. This takes more time to setup but is straightforward to operate and works especially well for drying flat stock. *I recommend that you create a direct contact vacuum drying system* and describe complete details of this method in the following pages.

Preparing wood for drying in a VacuPress4000 commercial vacuum kiln. Photo courtesy of Vacutherm, Inc.

Section 3: How to Build a Vacuum Kiln

Required

- Vacuum pump
- Vacuum chamber
- End plates
- Valves & gauge
- Heater
- Temperature controller
- Temperature sensor
- Electrical socket
- Shelf
- Moisture meter

Optional

- Fan
- Moisture trap
- Drain
- Clamps
- Programmable timer
- Solenoid valve

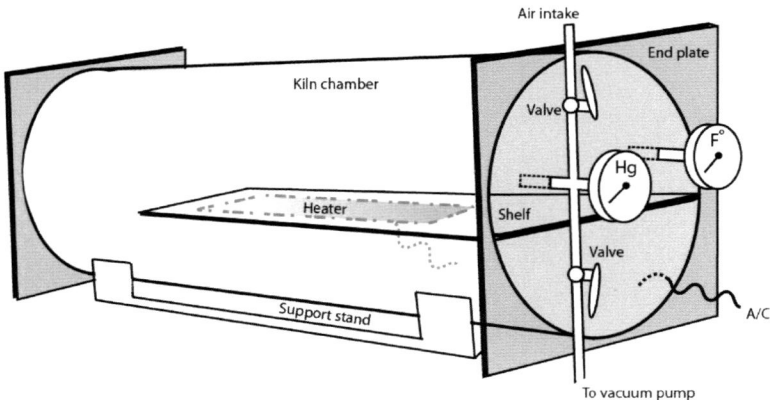

Fig. 3.0 – Illustration of the main elements for a wood drying vacuum kiln system.

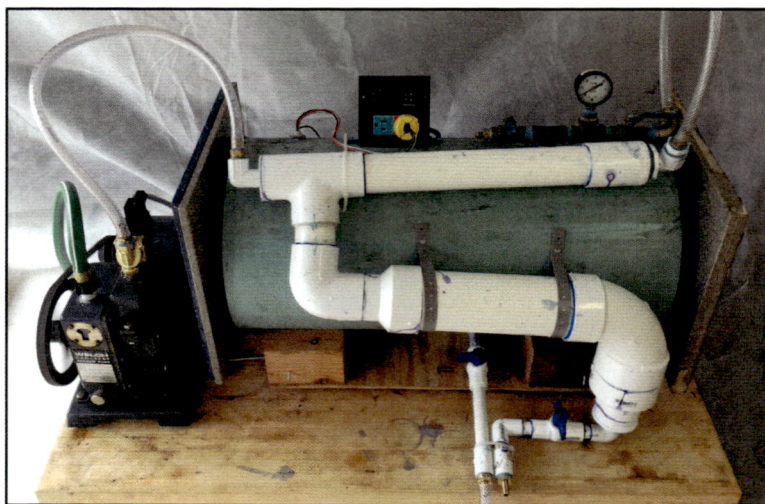

Fig. 3.1 – Exterior view of my vacuum kiln. The lower photo shows an optional moisture trap and drainage tank added to the system.

Details of required items

Let's take a detailed look at each of the items that comprise the vacuum kiln setup.

Vacuum pump

The critical factor in choosing a vacuum pump is that it can attain at least 27 inHg though higher really is better. Vacuum pumps that woodturners commonly use for reverse chucking bowls as well as pumps for veneer work usually only achieve lower vacuum. For wood drying it is best to use a pump rated in the range of 29.9 inHg. Sometimes manufacturers only give the specification of their vacuum pump in mm or Torr. In that case, use the Comparison of Pressure Measurements table in Appendix IV to convert to inHg. In general, avoid pumps for hobby crafts and go with pumps used for scientific or industrial applications.

Vacuum pumps are one of two kinds:
1. Oil-free
2. Oil-sealed

Oil-free vacuum pumps are a newer technology used in applications where contamination from oil mist might ruin a project or when certain gasses (including water vapor) from the vacuum chamber cannot be allowed to react with the pump's oil. As such, they tend to be more expensive than oil-sealed pumps. They come in a wide variety of configurations: rotary vane, rocking piston, regenerative blower, diaphragm, scroll, linear and more.

Since I don't have any experience with oil-free pumps, I encourage you to consult with a retailer or manufacturer to determine which configurations will work best for this application. From a maintenance standpoint, with an oil-free vane pump, you'll eventually need to replace the vanes which is more expensive but required much less often than changing the oil and filter on a lubricated pump. There are also corrosion resistant pumps that likely need less maintenance as they are better able to handle moisture vapor and may be worth the extra expense.

Oil-sealed pumps have been around for decades and tend to be one of two kinds: rotary vane or rotary piston and either type can be 115V or 230V. The piston pumps are generally much louder—like the incessant buzz of an oil-less compressor motor—and tend to run hotter but they are often more compact. Vane pumps are quieter with more of a soft clickety-clack sound and have few wearing parts other than the sacrificial vanes.

I bought a used Welch Duo-Seal 1400 vane pump on eBay for $100 ten years ago, and it has been a good pump for this application because it produces a high vacuum, has a large oil reservoir to dilute contaminants, and a low pump RPM to minimize friction and wear. This and similar models (1405, 1402, 1376, 1397, 1374, 1399, 1380, and 1392) continue to be readily available on eBay in the $150 to $250 range.

That said, here are a few more details to consider before choosing this kind of vacuum pump:

Oil-based rotary vane pumps should not be turned off when pulling vacuum without first sealing off the chamber and bringing the pump to atmospheric pressure because the oil (which is the only thing separating the difference in pressure) can get pushed into the intake side of the pump or beyond. To prevent this, you should add another valve to vent the pump inlet to atmospheric pressure before stopping the pump. While recommended, it is not required and is something you may want to forgo since it both adds cost and limits the possibility of putting the whole system on a timer to cycle the pump for additional vacuum as needed (as will be explained later).

With oil-based vacuum pumps, it is helpful (though not required) for the pump to have a sight glass that allows you to see the oil level, color of the oil, and any moisture buildup that might be occurring as you run the pump. Although a clear tube from the chamber to the vacuum pump will also allow you to see moisture condensation entering the system, it won't give you a sense of the overall amount.

It is best to get an oil-sealed pump that is designed to run continuously and to warm up the pump before use (though it should not run for an extended period if not pulling vacuum). As it heats up it can more effectively discharge water vapor, preventing the oil and water from mixing.

If the pump has a gas ballast valve you can use it to reduce moisture buildup as the pump is running. However, this also reduces the pump's compression, so it is a good idea to get a pump capable of pulling vacuum in excess of 27 inHg to ensure there will be sufficient vacuum when using the ballast valve option.

Water vapor can also be reduced by adding an in-line moisture trap before the pump, as will be explained later. Without a trap, plan to change the oil at least once per drying cycle to keep the pump operating at peak efficiency and prolong its life.

Fig. 3.2 – Welch Duo-Seal 1400 vacuum pump. Note site glass window for oil level, clear inlet tube connected to brass solenoid valve, green garden hose exhaust tube and steel gas ballast valve (left and rear of garden hose connection).

One last point regarding oil-sealed vacuum pumps: It is important to route vacuum pump exhaust to the outdoors to keep the air in your shop from becoming toxic with oil vapor. Also, be sure to never restrict the pump's exhaust.

Common Question: Pumps 1

"How much of a problem is moisture for the pump?"

There is conflicting analysis of the effect moisture has on a typical vacuum pump. The oil does keep the parts coated and the moisture at bay to some extent but various factors of the material construction can determine its susceptibility and longevity. You will have to decide if the added cost of a pump that is rated to handle moisture is worth it to you. As preventative maintenance, you should change the pump's oil regularly. You can also put a moisture trap in-line and use the gas ballast feature although, with large amounts of moisture, some will still find its way into the oil.

"How often should I change the oil in my pump?"

The most important maintenance you can do for an oil-sealed pump is to frequently change the oil (and this should be done when the pump is hot). Normally you won't need to do this during a drying cycle unless you are taking in so much water that you see the oil chamber becoming full. In that case, you need to add a moisture trap in-line before the pump. In any case, be sure to change the oil after completing the drying cycle because moisture and contaminants cause a loss of efficiency and could eventually damage the pump.

Common Question: Pumps 2

"In your opinion, how crucial is the gas ballast option for a kiln drying application?"

The gas ballast is a type of exhaust vent available on some vacuum pumps. It prevents contamination of the pump's oil by allowing air and moisture coming from the chamber to bypass the oil. For this reason, keep it open when you first pull vacuum. It can also help moisture in the oil to escape which is why you may want to also leave it partially open during normal operation. If you run without it you can achieve higher vacuum but more moisture will stay in the pump. Then you'll need to change the oil more frequently (though it's best to change the oil at the end of your drying cycle anyway). Higher moisture exposure can reduce efficiency and longevity of the pump so it's worth having the gas ballast option unless your pump is the type not affected by moisture. Alternately if you use a moisture trap before the pump or only need to pull vacuum on the chamber at the beginning of a two or three day drying run a gas ballast would not be needed.

"Do I have to use a special brand of vacuum pump oil or is generic ok?"

Higher priced oil may be more refined, making it more pure, viscous and stable. This could help maintain the life of your pump and allow you to see cloudy contamination easier. However, I use generic pump oil and it seems fine for my inexpensive pump.

Common Question: Pumps 3

"I have a 3 HP vacuum pump. Would this pump be able to handle the vacuum kiln?"

The critical consideration in choosing a pump is its vacuum rating, not horsepower. HP is a factor indicating the relative efficiency of the pump that won't be much of an issue for smaller chambers. As an example, for piston vacuum pumps, a general rule is that about 1 HP is needed for each 20 CFM of air pumped. This will be different for other kinds of pumps. If a pump is underrated for the size of chamber, it will still likely achieve near its vacuum rating but it will take longer than the manufacturer's specification.

"What is the CFM flow of your pump?"

A new model Welch Duo-Seal 1400 is rated at 0.9 CFM. Think of CFM as how fast the air can be removed from a chamber. For this application, the rate is not as important as the maximum attainable vacuum. Still, all pumps have internal leakage and do not achieve their ultimate rating, plus higher altitude and any small leaks in the chamber are further reasons to choose a pump capable of higher CFM. It's fine to use larger pumps on small systems but the reverse can cause your pump to wear out prematurely.

"I'd like to make a kiln big enough to dry 8 ft. boards. Is the Welch Duo-Seal 1400 sufficient for this?"

When designing larger chambers, try to minimize any extra space so the pump is only pulling necessary volume. Even with large containers, an undersized pump could very well achieve the desired vacuum keeping in mind the issues discussed above.

Vacuum chamber

For large, *commercial* vacuum kiln drying systems, the chamber is one of the most expensive parts because of the mechanical requirements for strength and preventing leakage. A relatively inexpensive solution for smaller scale drying is PVC pipe.

The one I used was 13" diameter Schedule 80 with 0.75" thick walls—a common throw-away from construction sites. The same diameter Schedule 40 PVC pipe is less than 0.44" thick and is also generally considered ok for vacuum though I haven't tried it. In either case, be sure to use solid core and *not* ABS (foam core) or styrene PVC, which will *not* be strong enough to withstand the forces created by the vacuum. You can learn more about PVC by reading the

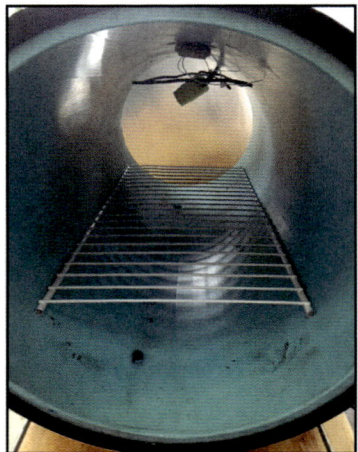

Fig. 3.3 – A view inside the vacuum chamber with drying shelf, electrical socket and bell jar gaskets installed.

specifications set forth in ASTM D1785 or by using the links provided in the Online Resources page (see Appendix V).

If you're thinking about making a chamber from another material, keep in mind that a cylinder has much greater structural strength than a cube, which would need considerably thicker walls for vacuum applications. If you don't want to scavenge PVC from a construction site, call around to plumbing suppliers to see what they can get or check with vacuum chamber suppliers provided in the Online Resources page.

Assuming you decide to make your own chamber from PVC, it is important to cut the ends of the PVC pipe as true as possible. You will then need to sand or file them completely flat to ensure a good seal with the end plates. A large disc sander can make quick work of that task.

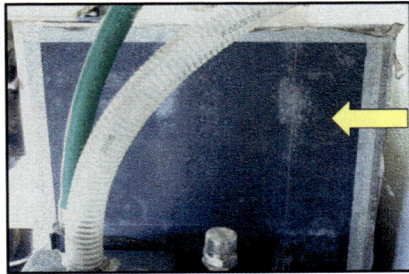

Fig. 3.4 – The arrow points to sandpaper attached to the end plate, creating a large sanding block handy for truing-up the PVC pipe.

Alternately, you can tape a sheet of sandpaper onto your end plate and use that as a large sanding block. (See Fig. 3.4)

Common Question: Chambers

"What is the biggest kiln you've seen made using the example in your book?"

The largest vacuum kiln like mine that I've seen is a 24" diameter tube about 4' length with steel end plates. Due to the size and weight (especially loaded) it sits on the floor. Others have told me of plans to weld a large metal container, or convert a 1000–gallon anhydrous ammonia tank, but I haven't seen pictures yet. The details in this book are intended for smaller non–commercial setups.

End plates

To seal the chamber, the end plates need to be made from a material with appropriate wall thickness and structural strength to prevent implosion. You should consult a mechanical engineer to ensure your end plates will not pose a safety hazard given the size of your chamber.

Fig. 3.5 – A Corian end plate and rubber bell jar gasket seals the PVC chamber.

That said, while an undersized material seems like it might implode or cause the chamber to takeoff like a rocket engine, I've never heard of either of those happening. Unless the end plate material is extremely brittle or breakable (like glass), what would likely happen is the end plate will bow to the point at which air leaks into the chamber, equalizing the atmospheric pressure almost instantly.

Clear end plates are useful if you need to see inside the chamber (for reading a thermometer or using your kiln to stabilize wood with resin). Glass is one option but a bit pricey for the required thickness and the most dangerous in the event of an implosion. Polycarbonate or acrylic sheet with the appropriate thickness would be a safer choice. Steel plate is economical if you are planning a larger chamber but be sure to spray with rust-proof enamel paint to keep the steel from rusting (brush strokes may not be flat enough for a good seal). Multiple layers of high quality plywood could also be used if appropriately sealed.

If using a PVC chamber then PVC sheet would be the best option for a permanently sealed end plate since you can chemically fuse them together using PVC primer and cement. PVC Type 2 sheet is a little stronger than Type 1 so get that if you can. Approximate thickness to use: ¾" sheet for a 12" cylinder, 1.5" for an 18" cylinder and 3" for a 24" diameter. Again, please consult a mechanical engineer to confirm the safety for your particular setup. For my 13" diameter kiln, I glued together a couple pieces of ½" Corian that were free off-cuts from a local supplier (see Fig. 3.6).

Rubber seals for the end plates keep the chamber from leaking. You can get bell jar gaskets (also called "L-gaskets") sized for your container or buy neoprene rubber sheet from the local hardware store. Generally, 1/8" thickness should be sufficient depending on the density of the material and the flatness of the ends of your chamber and end plates. You can go with thicker material if you need to "fill the gaps" or, if your

Fig. 3.6 – A sheet of neoprene rubber can also be added to the end plate.

ends are very flat, you may find that inner tube rubber from a tire similarly sized to the diameter of your kiln is perfectly fine.

If the ends of the chamber are cut true and the end plates are strong and flat, the chamber will easily seal when you draw vacuum. Otherwise you may need to use Dow Corning™ High Vacuum Grease on the gaskets to improve the seal. To add additional strength to the end plates and increase sealing pressure, clamps can also be used.

Valves & gauge

A couple of gas-rated plumbing ball valves with appropriate copper fittings are used to control the air intake and vacuum draw. For the connection through the chamber, you can either

Fig 3.7 – The valve on the right seals off the chamber from the vacuum pump. The valve on the left provides a way to bring air back into the chamber. The vacuum gauge is positioned between these two valves.

drill through the tube wall (as in Fig. 3.1) or through the end plate (as in Fig. 3.0). In the latter case, you may want to attach the hardware to a permanently sealed end plate so you don't have to juggle the extra weight or inadvertently loosen any of the connections.

After you drill holes you can glue parts in place with epoxy or polyurethane glue (i.e.: Gorilla Glue®) which will expand to fill any gaps. But you may get a better seal and have more flexibility to change your setup if you drill and cut threads. Cutting the threads isn't as hard as it sounds. You can buy a metal plug or an extra brass fitting with the same thread size as the ones you need to cut. Taper the leading threads with a grinding wheel. If cutting into material harder than PVC you may want to use a hacksaw to cut 2, 3 or 4 vertical V-shaped grooves running across the threads. Then, use locking vice-grips as a handle, keep the tap perfectly perpendicular and slowly turn it into the hole as you apply downward pressure.

To seal metal-to-metal connections, use brush-on sealant, such as RectorSeal® or Loctite® 592. Metal-to-plastic threaded connections can be sealed with RectorSeal® or Seal-All® contact adhesive. Holes made for wiring pass-through can be sealed with one of the Permatex® silicone vacuum sealants. Products that are rated for high vacuum applications typically have less outgassing of solvents which results in better vacuum initially. Note that Teflon tape is *not recommended* for any connections in vacuum applications.

A gauge to measure vacuum is essential. Not only does it show how the pump is performing, it can also help troubleshoot leaks in the chamber or other

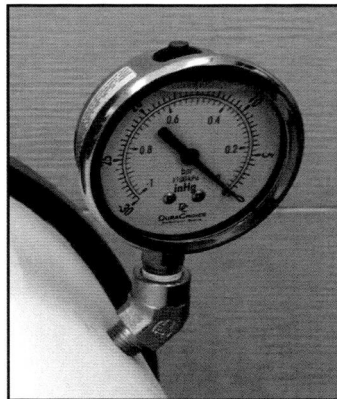

Fig 3.8 – A vacuum gauge can be directly threaded to the chamber. Photo courtesy of Conestoga Works.

connections. Vacuum gauges are inexpensive but not very accurate, as readings are subject to altitude, temperature and changes in atmospheric pressure due to weather. Moreover, they typically cannot be calibrated. A precision vacuum gauge, also called a "digital absolute pressure gauge" does not have these issues but is quite expensive. The standard dial gauge, despite its shortcomings, will suffice for the requirements at hand.

Common Question: Gauges

"My vacuum gauge doesn't point to zero. Is there a way to fix it?"

You can reset a vacuum gauge by inserting a small pin under the rubber stopper on the top of the gauge or by using the small pop-up button (if included) on the top of the gauge. This will release the internal pressure that may have developed during shipment.

"My vacuum gauge has an air bubble in it. Is it broken?"

Vacuum gauges that are filled with glycerin always have an air bubble inside. This is normal and doesn't impact the proper functionality.

Common Question: Sealants

"Which sealants should I use to connect the various parts?"

There are a lot of choices and many will do a good job. The ones rated for high vacuum are generally very expensive. Here are some affordable options:

• Weldon® 780 PVC Cement and Weldon PVC Primer can be used to form a chemical bond for PVC slip connections.

• Rectorseal® Tru-Blu™ Pipe Thread Sealant is good for metal and PVC threads. It remains flexible when set and is intended for high vibration environments.

• Loctite® 592 Slow Cure Thread Sealant is considered a good choice for metal pipe threads by the vacuum industry. It is not recommended for plastic (PVC).

• Loctite® 569 Hydraulic Thread Sealant is a more expensive option that can be used for both metal and PVC and is suited for vibration.

• Seal-All® Contact Adhesive and Sealant is good for sealing threaded metal to plastic connections through holes cut in the pipe. Although too viscous for vertical applications, it has a quick setup time and may also be used to seal leaks.

• Permatex® offers a high torque, a high temp, and a general RTV silicone vacuum sealant, each with unique characteristics and applications. Although silicone is considered to have a relatively high gas permeability, RTV silicone sealants cure quickly and can be used in vertical applications to provide a good seal that can also be cleanly and easily removed if necessary.

• Dow Corning® High Vacuum Grease is good for rubber and O-ring connections and is generally used when an impermanent seal is required.

Heater

The heat source will need to evenly heat all the pieces of wood you put in the chamber. Whether you plan to dry flat boards, round lathe-turned wood, or other shapes or types of material will influence which approach to use. The different methods are correlated with the way heat can be transferred:

- *Convection* – This is the slowest form of heat transfer. More importantly, convection becomes less effective as vacuum increases so the load needs to be heated while some air is present in the chamber.

- *Radiation* – This works for various shaped items if each piece can be placed equidistant from the heat source. Multiple heat sources around the wood will provide the most uniform heat.

- *Conduction* – This is the best choice for quickly and evenly heating flat pieces of wood. Heat mats can be placed between layers and aluminum sheeting can be used to distribute the heat more uniformly and across larger areas.

Convection heating

The combination of a light bulb and small fan connected to a thermostat is a functional and inexpensive convection setup (see Fig. 3.9). Start with a low wattage light bulb or Chromalox® Edison screw-base heater placed centrally away from the chamber walls, so as not to risk melting the chamber. I also recommend shielding a PVC chamber with aluminum sheet to prevent melting from hot-spots.

Fig. 3.9 – *The top arrow points out the thermostat. Middle arrow is a light bulb. Bottom arrow is small computer fan. The bulb and fan are automatically turned on/off together by the thermostat depending on the temperature.*

Keep the heat source equidistant from all pieces you are drying and use a small fan to help evenly distribute the heat.

There are a few downsides of using convection heating: It can be difficult to evenly heat the load. The whole interior of the chamber becomes equally heated, which limits the ability to condense the moisture inside the kiln. It also requires a discontinuous vacuum cycle which can be more challenging to run because of the need to juggle between the vacuum and heating requirements.

Radiation heating

For radiation based heating, light bulbs could be used, but would be need to be arranged in a way that every piece of wood is uniformly illuminated in order to receive an equal amount of heat. Another option for radiation heat is an infrared ceramic heat emitter (typically used for reptiles or farm animals) but be sure to confirm the maximum temperature it can achieve as many are too low. For larger installations, infrared sauna heaters could be utilized.

Due to the limitation of convection and radiation heating for our application, I recommend the following approach using conduction heat.

Conduction heating

If you primarily dry flat wood, heat pads from the local drug store in conjunction with aluminum sheeting from the hardware store will disperse heat evenly across your lumber. They are relatively inexpensive and include a built-in rheostat to control the amount of heat. However, be sure to completely weigh them down or they will crumple-up under vacuum and become useless for future loads (and possibly a fire hazard).

Rubber or silicone coated heat mats are really the *best option* and are sold for various uses. The most common ones are for keeping seeds, plants, feet, pets or livestock warm, preventing outdoor pipes or engines from freezing, heating the bed of a 3D printer, as well as for bending wood. They distribute very even

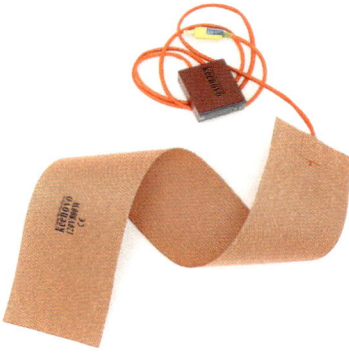

Fig. 3.10 – *A flexible silicone heater made can be used flat or wrapped onto rounded objects. Photo courtesy of Keenovo*

heat that can be precisely controlled. They do not scrunch up under vacuum like the drug store heat pads but do cost more. Some heat mats are sold with a built-in temperature sensor (thermistor) and include a digital temperature controller for regulating the amount of heat. Check the temperature ratings to be sure it can achieve at least 110ºF (43ºC).

For larger setups, you might also consider the resistance grids used to heat floors. The typical ceramic tile bathroom installation uses electric radiant heat embedded in mortar so you'll have to come up with another way to hold everything in place. Other radiant grids come in rolls, such as for use under floating wood flooring. Typically, they are sold with thermostats rated for specific installations. You will need to do some research to determine which product is appropriate for your larger setup.

Whichever heat source you use, you will need to set a thermostat, temperature controller or rheostat to control the temperature. The exception to this would be a heater with a maximum temperature of 110ºF (43ºC) to 130ºF (55ºC) in which case you could technically get by without one. For example, I have a CozyWinters foot-warming mat that is rated to 135ºF (57ºC) but actually only reaches 100ºF to 110ºF (43ºC). So, this could be used without the need to regulate the temperature. On the other hand, I also have a Keenovo silicone heater mat that will quickly go to 240°F (115°C) in less than a minute. This would absolutely need to be regulated in order to prevent the wood from cracking, or the kiln, rack or other parts from melting.

Some kiln loads will need to have more than one heat mat to evenly heat the lumber. In this case, a single temperature controller connected to one mat can still be used as long as all the mats are the same type and powered on and off together.

To facilitate switching between different types of heaters for different kinds of lumber, you can attach mating connectors to the temperature sensor wires inside the chamber (that originate from the controller unit) with the wires from each mat's thermistor. For example, a 2.1mm x 5.5mm 12V DC plug with screw terminals is easy and inexpensive.

Fig. 3.11 – DC connectors for each temperature sensor allow for an easy swap to the controller.

Note: An additional pair of wires and connector will be needed if you plan to use a separate temperature probe for measuring the heat inside the wood. (The need for this is further explained in the Temperature Sensor section below.)

Common Question: Heat 1

"If the vapor pressure of water at 69°F is 29.22 inHg, why do I have to heat the wood at all?"

Exactly how water behaves inside the cell structure of wood while under the influence of heat and vacuum is a complex topic and my understanding is limited. It seems that without heat the moisture in the wood is not accessible to react in the same way. I do know that the method I describe here works well and using heat to dry wood in a vacuum is the industry standard. Feel free to experiment without heat and let me know your results.

"Why can't I just heat the entire chamber from the outside?"

This doesn't work due in part to the limited convection (air) inside the chamber. The wood may never reach the required temperature. It's also better to have a temperature differential between the wood and the surrounding atmosphere to condense the moisture vapor.

"What temperature should I heat to?"

The temperature needed depends primarily on the level of vacuum achieved. Higher vacuum will allow lower heat. (See the Boiling Point of Water graph in Appendix IV.) The interior of the wood will likely need to reach 100° to 110°F and that may require exterior heating of 120°F or more depending on the thickness. But it's also important to limit the maximum temperature to avoid overheating, which may cause cracking, and to keep the heat below the maximum operating temperature of your chamber material. For both Schedule 40 and 80 PVC that is 140°F.

Common Question: Heat 2

"How long does it take to heat the wood to 110°F?"

The time it takes to heat the wood depends on the thickness and density of the wood and even more so with the heating method you use. Radiation with complete line-of-sight coverage or conduction using heat pads in direct contact with the surface of the wood might take an hour or two. Convection will be much slower and could take half of a day or more. You should not rush this process by using a strong heat source (such as a high wattage light bulb or high voltage heat mat), which could cause the wood to crack. Instead, use a slow and steady approach.

"What wattage heat mat is required?"

Wattage determines how quickly the mat heats which is not that important for our application. Instead, the main factor is to locate one capable of producing at least 110°F to 130°F and then maintaining that using a temperature controller. The best approach is to heat evenly which can be facilitated by adding aluminum sheet between the heat mat and the wood. You may also need several mats to uniformly heat the entire load.

"If I use a light bulb for my heat source, what wattage should I use?"

The wattage in this situation is important: If you use too little, depending on the heat loss of your chamber, the wood might never reach 110°F. Too much can produce uneven heating that might crack the wood. Be patient as the wood is brought to temperature. The chamber size and load will determine if you need one or several bulbs.

Temperature controller

It is essential to precisely control the heat applied to the wood. A voltage transformer can be used to limit the heat mat to the desired temperature. Alternately, an inexpensive rheostat can be used for light bulbs or other low voltage heaters. While these might be more expensive than a digital temperature controller, they don't require particular wiring and other small parts to implement and will provide consistent rather than cycling heat. Set the voltage based on a thermometer reading placed inside the kiln or a temperature sensor inside the wood.

Fig. 3.12 – This Variac® voltage transformer can control the temperature of whatever heat source is plugged into it.

Fig. 3.13 – A digital temperature controller with thermistor (on top) is an economical and versatile thermostat.

Alternately, digital temperature controllers for heating and cooling are surprisingly affordable since they are used in so many industries. They are often sold with a temperature sensor included making them versatile thermostats. This will automatically turn the heater on and off based on the temperature of the sensor, which can be placed in various locations including *inside* the wood (see next topic for further considerations). You will need to connect a few wires and program a few settings to get it working but it is a straightforward procedure detailed in Appendix II.

Temperature sensor

The best option for measuring temperature is to use a sensor called a thermistor – an electric resistor whose resistance depends on temperature. They are small and inexpensive and used in a variety of electronics such as toasters, computers, refrigerators and pretty much anything where temperature needs to be monitored.

A thermistor can simply provide a temperature reading or, when combined with a temperature controller, can function as a thermostat and control the temperature inside the kiln by turning on and off the heat source.

Since wood is a good insulating material, the temperature in the center of the wood will remain lower than the heat at the surface or in the chamber. Depending on the thickness and type of lumber, a difference of 10°F might by typical. Knowing this might allow you to simply guestimate the proper heat setting based on a thermometer inside the kiln. Another approach would be to use a temperature probe with its own readout to monitor the temperature inside the wood. You would still need to manually adjust the heater accordingly.

With a certain arrangement, a sensor inside the wood could be used to automatically adjust the heater. This would be the most precise way to ensure that the necessary temperature for drying is achieved. The initial problem with this arrangement is that it takes a considerable amount of time for the interior of a piece of wood to reach the target

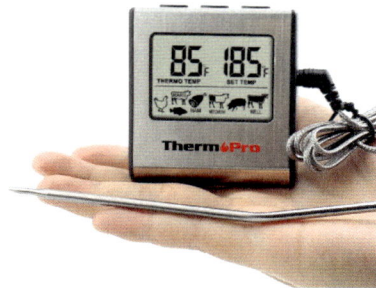

Fig. 3.14 – A cooking thermometer with probe can be used to directly monitor temperature inside the wood. Photo courtesy of ThermoPro.

temperature during which the heater would reach very high temperatures causing the outside of the wood to overheat and crack.

Unless you use a heat source that inherently cannot go above 130ºF (54ºC), you would need to use a voltage transformer (such as the Variac® mentioned above) to limit the heat mat to the desired temperature. Another option is to add a second temperature controller connected to a sensor on the heater surface (or thermistor built into the mat) that will limit the heater while the wood is being brought up to temperature. A diagram of this arrangement is shown in Figure 3.15.

The method you choose will depend on various factors: for example, the type of lumber you plan to dry may determine the way that you heat it which in turn may determine the way you measure temperature in the kiln or wood. The overall cost and the items you already have on hand may also be a determining factor. Sections 4 and 5 will further elucidate these approaches.

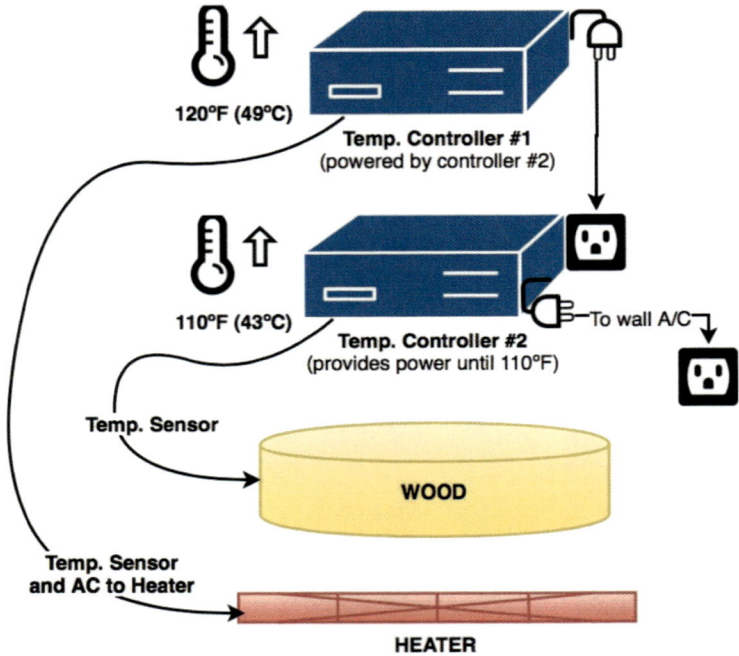

120°F (49°C)

Temp. Controller #1
(powered by controller #2)

110°F (43°C)

Temp. Controller #2
(provides power until 110°F)

To wall A/C

Temp. Sensor

WOOD

**Temp. Sensor
and AC to Heater**

HEATER

Fig. 3.15 – Individually controlling the temperature of the wood and the heater is the most precise way to achieve quality results. In this arrangement, the lumber is heated to the desired temperature by a controller set only slightly higher than the target temperature and activated by a separate controller that monitors a sensor inside the wood. Wiring diagrams for this setup can be found in Appendix II.

Electrical socket

An electrical connection inside the kiln is needed to run the heating element. You may prefer to run this through the end plate instead of the chamber wall. In either case, the electrical components need to be placed high up in the chamber with some thought given to cable management in order to keep electricity away from any water that may collect in the chamber. Be sure to use solid (not stranded) copper wire and remove the outer sheath of the wire bundle to prevent leaks. Use RTV silicone or other appropriate sealant to fill the hole, making sure to fill the gaps between the wires as well.

Shelf

A shelf or two is needed to support the wood being dried. The placement can help ensure each piece receives consistent heat and airflow. Since water will collect at the bottom of the chamber, the shelf is also important to keep the wood, heating element, electrical cords and any other items inside the kiln above the water.

Moisture meter

You'll need to have a way to quickly and precisely measure the percentage of moisture in your material. An inexpensive two-pin moisture meter for wood is fine. Look for one that gives you a range of at least 6% to 24%, has a display resolution and accuracy of 1% or smaller and uses a standard type of battery. Newer models have digital displays with a larger testing range of 2% to 70% and greater accuracy of about 0.5%.

The pin type meters use electric resistance to determine MC. I recommended inserting the pins parallel to the grain for greatest accuracy. If the pins are inserted across the grain the meter may read 1 to 2% too low. Temperature of the wood can also impact the reading 1 to 2%. A very rough correction to compensate for temperature is to subtract 1% for every 20ºF (6.6ºC) the wood is above 70ºF (21ºC), or to add 1% for every 20ºF below 70ºF.

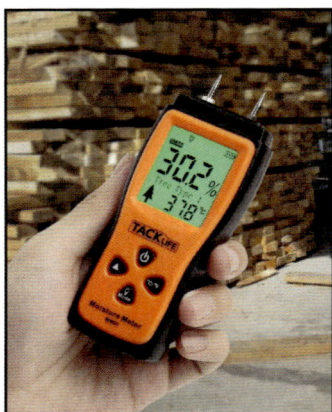

Fig. 3.16 – A two-prong moisture meter uses electrical resistance to instantly indicate the percentage of moisture in the wood. Photo courtesy of Tacklife.

Even though pin type meters cannot accurately read MC of wood fibers deeper than 0.25", the physics of drying wood in a vacuum kiln causes an equalizing of moisture content from the core to the surface of wood, so the MC reading at the outside will be very similar to the MC on the inside after drying in the vacuum kiln.

Dielectric (radio frequency) moisture meters use surface contact flat plate electrodes that do not penetrate the wood. They have a similar accuracy to resistance meters but are not affected by temperature variations. They can be used with any side grain orientation but not end grain. Some require that you perform a correction to compensate for the different density between wood species. Others have the corrections built into the circuitry. Since there can be a lot of normal density variation within each species, the accuracy of dielectric meters can be limited. For this reason, I recommend a resistance moisture meter but either one will get the job done.

Another way to know if a piece of wood is "dry" is to keep track of its weight over time. When the weight becomes constant over several months of air-drying, it has dried to the ambient environment. While only appropriate for pieces easily weighed, this method never provides the actual MC value and its relative measurements could easily allow going beyond the target MC when vacuum kiln drying (since the piece will continue to lose weight all the way down to 0% MC). A moisture meter provides an instant measurement and you can also use it to check different parts of any size piece—including the interior after cutting a board, block or log.

Details of optional items

Fan

A fan is useful in a couple of scenarios: First, if you plan to use convection heating, a small fan *inside* the chamber is helpful to distribute heat evenly around the wood. Connect it to the same thermostat controlled outlet that cycles the heat source. Second, if you use conduction heating, a fan can be used to cool the *exterior* of the kiln walls. This will help condense the relatively warm moisture vapor back to a liquid inside the chamber. In this situation, the fan's effectiveness will be limited by the external ambient temperature as compared with the internal temperature.

Moisture trap

Depending on the size and moisture content of the wood being dried, you might extract anywhere from a cup to a gallon of water (or more for large chambers). The easiest way to prevent this from entering your pump is to build a very tight chamber with no leakage and only use the pump to draw the vacuum at the beginning of the 2 to 3-day drying cycle. While this is possible, it is more common to have to top-off the vacuum throughout the drying cycle. Unless the moisture vapor in the kiln has condensed to a liquid, drawing vacuum during the drying process will bring moisture vapor from the chamber into your pump.

To minimize the amount of moisture entering the pump, you can add a moisture trap inline between the chamber and pump. This will extend the life of the pump and require fewer oil changes. Some vacuum pumps are designed to run with a gas ballast feature that allows

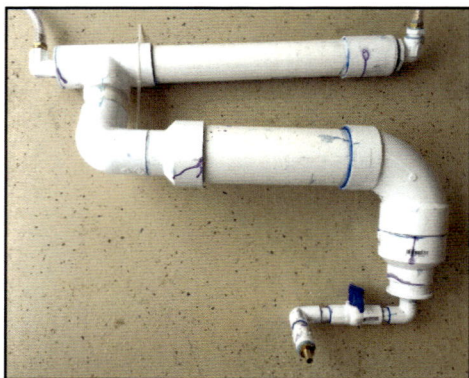

Fig. 3.17 – A homemade moisture trap and drain tank using Schedule 40 PVC pipe. This can be completely separated from the vacuum chamber if necessary.

moisture in the pump to escape. Others are impervious to moisture. In those cases, the trap is not needed. Otherwise, I recommend adding it.

Traps go by a few different names: water trap, moisture trap, liquid trap and cold trap all essentially do the same thing, but there are a few different approaches.

Fig. 3.18 – A section of the moisture trap revealing Raschig rings inside. These provide a large surface area and complex airflow path to promote condensation of the moisture vapor.

The approach I recommend is to add additional PVC pipe and loosely but completely fill it with one of these options (listed in order of effectiveness) – ceramic Raschig rings, copper mesh, plastic beads, or even pieces of plastic drinking straws. (See Fig. 3.18) Then add a pathway for the moisture to flow and a way to collect it. This entire setup can be added later if needed and completely removed if no longer necessary. (See Fig. 3.17)

Another type of in-line trap is a canister with desiccant that absorbs moisture. You will need a way to heat the moisture out of the desiccant when it becomes saturated (a heating element may be included in the unit itself) or simply replace with new desiccant. I haven't personally used this approach, and it seems it might be limited for the quantities of moisture we are dealing with here, but it could be the right solution for small loads with low moisture content. Other traps utilize electricity or dry ice or additional methods you can research online.

As noted earlier, condensation naturally occurs when the chamber walls are relatively cool compared to the heated moisture vapor escaping the wood. To promote this condensation, reduce the temperature of the kiln walls using air conditioning or cooling fans on the exterior. When successful, you may find that a moisture trap is not needed as water can just be collected from the bottom of the kiln.

Whichever method you use, the good news is that once the moisture vapor has condensed back to a liquid it will not be able to enter your vacuum pump.

Drain

A considerable amount of moisture can collect at the bottom of the chamber during the drying cycle. You can put the kiln on an incline and have a tray or bucket ready to collect this water when you open the end plate. However, it is more convenient to be able to drain the water *before* removing the end plates.

Fig. 3.19 – Drain pipe located at the bottom of the chamber provides a way to remove water from the chamber.

To do this, add a hole at the bottom of your chamber and attach an external drain line using metal or PVC pipe and a ball valve. (See Fig. 3.19) With this arrangement you will need to release the vacuum on the chamber *before* opening the drain.

If you don't want to lose vacuum when draining off the water, you will need to add a secondary water collection area – such as PVC pipe or a long section of reinforced 3/8" ID tubing – with a valve on both ends. When first pulling vacuum on the chamber, also pull vacuum in this secondary area. After water collects in the kiln, open the top valve and let gravity fill this section. Then close off the top valve at which point the water can be drained using the bottom valve. (See Fig. 3.20)

Fig. 3.20 – A drain and additional tubing with secondary valve allows for removal of water while maintaining vacuum.

Now let's take a moment to state the obvious: since considerable water may collect inside the chamber, be extra careful with the placement of the various electrical wires as this can be a *very dangerous* combination!

If you plan to dry only small loads, I recommend that you wait and add the drain later only if needed as it increases potential for vacuum leakage of the chamber.

Clamps

Two, three or four bar clamps may be useful to help to seal the chamber tightly enough to initiate vacuum. Other types of clamps, latches or threaded bolts could also be utilized. In addition to sealing the end plate, they can also help strengthen it by counteracting the bowing that may occur under high levels of vacuum.

Fig. 3.21 – Bar clamps secure the end plates.

Programmable timer

A chamber cannot endlessly hold vacuum. Once you determine how often it requires additional vacuum, a programmable timer can be set to cycle the vacuum pump on and off. If your chamber holds vacuum in the necessary range for a few days, or you prefer to manually top-off the chamber when required, then you won't need the timer.

Solenoid valve

If you need to cycle the pump during drying, and you do so automatically using a timer, then you will probably want to add a solenoid valve that will automatically open and close at the same time. This can be either in addition to or in place of the manual valve that seals off the chamber. A "normally closed" solenoid valve will open when the timer comes on and, when powered together with the pump, will top-off the chamber vacuum. This also has the advantage of being able to seal off the chamber from the vacuum pump which can leak vacuum when not running.

Fig. 3.22 – A solenoid valve can automatically open when power is applied. Photo courtesy of EhcoTech Intl.

Vacuum-rated solenoid valves can be expensive but gas-rated ones are sufficient since any leakage can be compensated for by cycling the pump with the programmable timer. A 12V DC adaptor or AC power cord will be needed to power the unit depending on which model you choose. Be sure to orient the flow arrow on the unit pointing back to the kiln to get a better seal when the pump is off and the valve is closed.

Assembly and troubleshooting

It may take several days with the vacuum pump running to fully de-gas the chamber from the epoxy, caulk and other solvents used to create your vacuum chamber. Your vacuum will improve after this initial de-gassing period, except for the fact that the oil in your pump (if you have an oil-based pump) is now contaminated by this residue. If you'd like to see the maximum vacuum the system can produce, you will need to replace it with fresh oil. If you are seeing unusually low vacuum gauge readings or cannot get a vacuum reading at all, you may have a leak.

If you can't get any vacuum, first check the pump by covering the tubing or inlet hole to make sure vacuum is being drawn. Then check to make sure the end plates are very tightly fit. You may need to add thicker gaskets or some bar clamps to improve the seal.

If you have low vacuum from a large leak, you can try locating it by tightly surrounding the chamber with a full bag of air. Then pull vacuum and watch where the bag starts to collapse. This can give you some general clues about the problem area and may be enough to indicate where a large leak is located. Use your hands to secure each suspicious spot while listening for the sound of the leak. Additionally, an ultrasonic leak detector can be used to locate small leaks that are otherwise inaudible. (It converts the sound of the leak to an audible level and provides a visual readout on an LED meter.)

To find very small leaks, pull the strongest vacuum on the chamber you can. Note the vacuum gauge reading. Then spray isopropyl alcohol (85% drug store type is ok) around the chamber one area at a time. When the isopropyl alcohol gets sucked into the chamber, the gauge will indicate a drop in vacuum.

Another approach is to apply a small amount of somewhat viscous sealant around all the connections as you pull vacuum and watch where it gets sucked in. Release the vacuum, apply more sealant to the offending connection and let it dry overnight. If you can't locate any spots where a leak is apparent, the vacuum may have pulled the sealant into the void sealing the leak. Again, allow it to set overnight and see if the problem is solved.

Some sealant options include: Rectorseal® Tru-Blu™, Seal-All® Contact Adhesive and Sealant, Permatex® RTV Silicone Vacuum Sealant, or Dow Corning® High Vacuum Grease (for impermanent connections). Other "leak stop" sprays and brush-on products as well as specially formulated low vapor pressure epoxy resin sealants can also be used.

Strive to have the chamber hold maximum vacuum for at least 24 hours with minimal loss (1/2 to 1 inHg). This is definitely attainable if you have carefully constructed your kiln and used the recommended sealants.

Cost to build

The total cost for my vacuum kiln setup was a bit under $500. Could you do it for less? Sure! My setup included several optional items and a few others could have been purchased online at a discount. Might it cost you more? Absolutely!

Depending on your needs, you can create a very small but complete vacuum kiln drying system for under $200 or a large, elaborate one for under $1000. (Compared to a *used* commercial vacuum kiln I found on eBay priced at $16,000 it's all relative!)

The next section will show an assortment of vacuum kilns that demonstrate this cost range.

Commercial vacuum kilns come up on the used market every so often. Even then, they are expensive, very large, and more than you'll ever need for a typical woodworking hobby.

Section 4: Additional Vacuum Kiln Examples

This section presents a few off-the-shelf chambers that could get you up and running quickly, along with several vacuum kilns made by people who customized the design in this book to suit their needs.

Pre-made vacuum kilns

Several pre-made and custom vacuum kilns are available for purchase, with prices based mostly on size and added hardware. For nearly all the options presented below, you will still need to add a heating element, temperature controller, electrical connection and shelf, as well as a vacuum pump.

A completely transparent acrylic chamber is available from Abbess Instruments. They make a broad range of systems including custom options for mostly science and industrial applications. As such, pricing is higher than the other choices presented here.

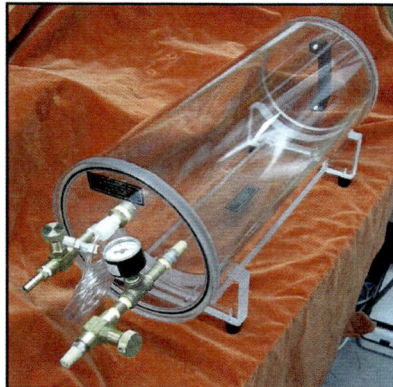

A transparent acrylic vacuum chamber by Abbess Instruments.

Wood stabilization chambers by Conestoga Works come in three sizes.

Conestoga Works offers transparent vacuum chambers for wood stabilization that could be modified for drying wood. These are available in 4", 6" or 8" diameter and are about 18" long. Prices currently range from $200 to $400.

Small vacuum chambers are available on eBay and Amazon in the $100 to $200 range. They are offered in a few different configurations and some even include a vacuum pump. You'll have to consider if there is enough room to fit everything that needs to be added inside the chamber including the size of wood you plan to dry. For the right situation, they are a great value.

Example of a small, affordable, ready-made vacuum chamber.

Conestoga Works is the first company I am aware of that offers a complete and affordable wood drying vacuum kiln intended for small scale woodworkers. It includes all the required elements other than a vacuum pump which they sell separately. The chambers are available in 12" or 18" diameter and can be made to custom lengths (a 24" length is shown in the photo). The heating system can also be customized with multiple pads and includes an

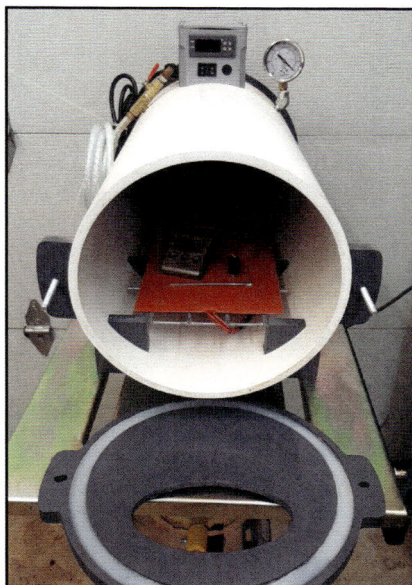

A Conestoga Works complete wood drying vacuum kiln system. Photo courtesy of Conestoga Works.

integrated temperature controller as well as a separate temperature sensing probe with digital readout to monitor the load. Pricing starts around $600.

Another option that is plug-n-play but is limited to drying small pieces is a vacuum oven. Although quite expensive when purchased new, you could find an affordable used one at a local university or laboratory surplus sale, or perhaps an auction specializing in medical and scientific equipment.

A vacuum oven provides a small insulated chamber with suitable heat for drying wood, plus an observation window, built-in thermometer, connector for the vacuum pump and air-intake, power cord, and internal shelf, all in a UL-rated tabletop unit. Perfect!

A professionally made vacuum oven by Napco.

One example is the Napco model 5831 that has an internal dimension slightly less than 8"W x 8"H x 12"D. A used one in working condition can be purchased on eBay in the $250 to $550 range. Larger capacity models are available at higher prices. You can then simply hook up an appropriate vacuum pump and begin drying.

Adaptations from readers of this book

End-Plate Connections Example

Here is a vacuum chamber made by Fred Connell. All the plumbing and electrical connections go through the end plate, keeping the chamber walls intact. This end may be permanently sealed. Diamond plate is readily available and comes in steel, stainless steel or aluminum. If using steel, the interior should be coated to

prevent rust. The clamps add additional strength to the end plates and will help keep them from bowing under vacuum.

In this photo, Fred demonstrates a precise way to cut the chamber edges perfectly flat. A compound X-Y table is used to position a router bit and a custom lathe steady-rest holds the chamber while allowing slow rotation by hand.

Smallest Example

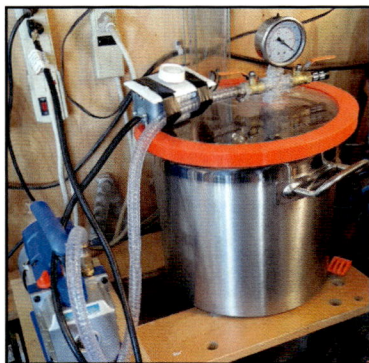

Al Collins knew he only needed to dry two or three box-sized blocks at a time. With limited shop space and budget for the project, he opted for an off-the-shelf eBay solution.

The five-gallon container is about 11" x 11" and uses a ¾" Plexiglas top. After adding a small lightbulb that hangs from the black polyester coated "hardware cloth" wire shelf, a rheostat to control the amount of heat, an oven thermometer, and the electrical connection, the total cost was still under $200, including the pump!

The heating in this system is primarily radiation with perhaps some conduction through the metal wire shelf.

Note the three solid-core electrical wires that pass through the top offer a leak-proof electrical connection. They are then spliced to a typical stranded wire AC power cable inside.

Convection Heat Example

This is the design presented in the first edition of this book. It uses discontinuous vacuum with a light bulb and small fan to disperse heat. A thermostat (top arrow) regulates the overall temperature and an exterior insulating blanket helps retain uniform heat throughout the chamber.

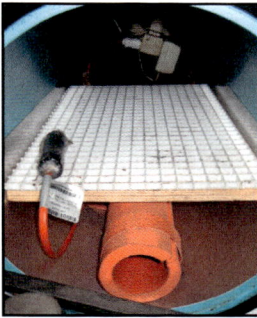

It works equally well with other heat sources including the pipe heater jacket shown here. Regardless of which heat source is used, if you have a PVC chamber, it is important to add aluminum sheet to help deflect and disperse heat and to keep the temperature below 140°F (60°C).

The convection approach is quick and inexpensive to setup but cycling vacuum and heat to achieve uniform temperature along with appropriate vacuum to successfully execute drying is more challenging than the conduction based heating method recommended in Section 3.

Sealed & Clear End-Plate Example

This vacuum kiln by Brian Jackson is 18" diameter and three feet long. One end is permanently sealed with PVC sheet (1.5" recommended). The other end utilizes a 1.25" clear acrylic sheet that shows some bowing due to vacuum. Brian says the thermostat on top is not really necessary as the kiln temperature never exceeds 100ºF (38ºC) using a CozyWinters heat mat. Since his pump generates 29.9 inHg it provides plenty of vacuum for successful drying at this lower temperature. The whole kiln is on a slight incline to allow water to run out into a tray when the front cover is removed. All penetrations of the main PVC tube are sealed with copious amounts of silicone. Despite the generally high gas permeability of silicone, it seems to be doing a very good job as Brian says the chamber holds vacuum for about a week, losing less than 2 inHg.

Hobbyist Goes Commercial

Charles Waggoner developed his vacuum drying kiln to the point of producing a small-scale commercial system that he now makes available to others through the Conestoga Works website.

An overview photo is shown in the Pre-Made Vacuum Kilns section above, so a couple detail photos are presented here.

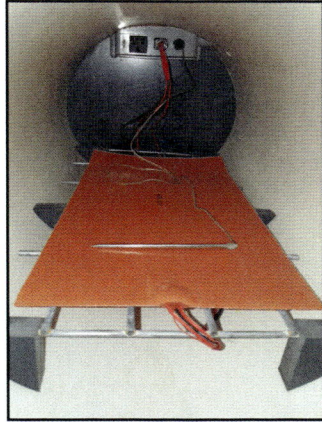

The industrial shelf is well stabilized and can easily support heavy loads. The heat mat and temperature sensor each have their own receptacles and the electrical layout is well thought out and neatly integrated.

A temperature probe is used to monitor the heat inside the wood (or anywhere you place the probe) but is not responsible for

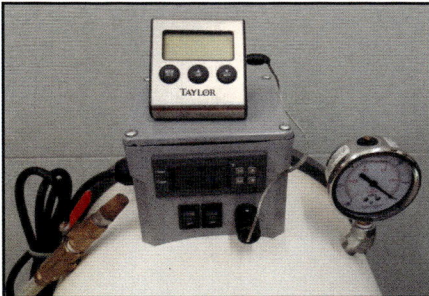

cycling the heater itself. This is a straightforward approach that isolates the probe to a purely informational function preventing any heating mishaps should it dislodge or malfunction.

Inspired Example

Many of the improvements Jeff Hankinson brought to my original vacuum kiln design are now incorporated in the current recommendations of this book.

Jeff provided labels for the various components in his kiln so most items are self-evident. (One note about the humidity gauge and moisture wires/pins seen in his photos: Jeff later reported that these didn't work reliably under vacuum and has since stopped using them.)

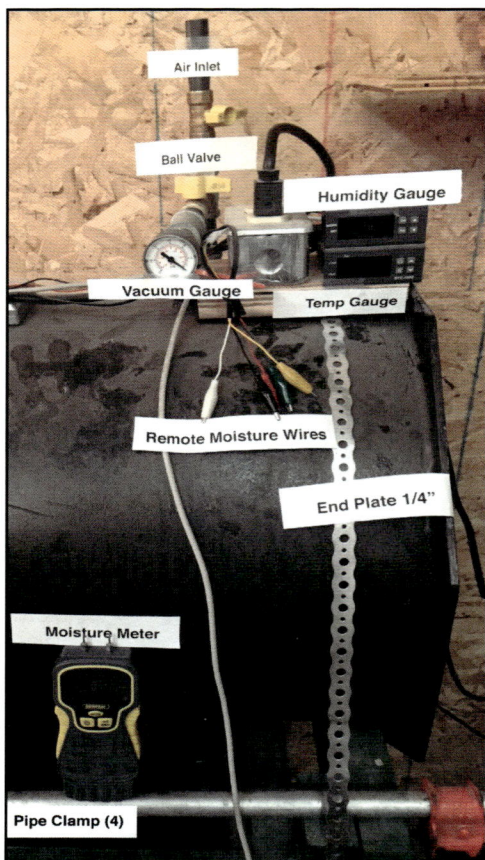

The steel chamber is sealed using a small bike tire inner tube cut around the circumference to make a thin flat doughnut gasket along with 14" x 14" x 1/4" steel plate (with the corners cut off to make an octagonal shape.) The other end is permanently welded closed.

Jeff generally dries multiple tiers of wood by creating "sandwich" layers of aluminum, heat mat, wood, heat mat, etc., providing heat to both the top and bottom of the wood.

He notes, "Consistent heating through the wood seems to be key to good results. To that end, I place my temperature sensor midway up the side of a piece in a hole about an inch deep." (You can see an example of this in the photo above in the square block of wood on the left.)

He cautions, "I try to keep the wood and mats away from the walls due to the large amount of condensation that runs down. Obviously, the wood would just soak it up again and get stained (don't ask how I know)."

Jeff came up with a way to condense the water vapor before it reaches the vacuum pump by adding in-line a small chamber filled with straws. He explains how he made it:

"I took a 9" section of 4.5" steel pipe, attached a 1/2" pipe nipple to flat plates to fit over the ends (about 5" square) and welded-on one of them. I also drilled and welded-on a pipe nipple to the side of the pipe near the welded-on bottom end plate, about an inch up from the bottom. I fit four lengths of threaded 5/16" rod to hold the top plate to the bottom and formed a gasket out of car tire inner tube. I glue-gunned a small round plastic mesh spacer with 3/4" 'legs' to fit in the pipe and put it on the bottom so that air moving from the side opening near the bottom could get in. Finally, I filled the pipe tightly with 8" drinking straws from the local dollar store – about 400 of them.

I plumbed it in-
line with the
vacuum pump,
tied the bottom
drain pipe to a
length of 1"
reinforced nylon
pipe with gas-
rated ball valves at

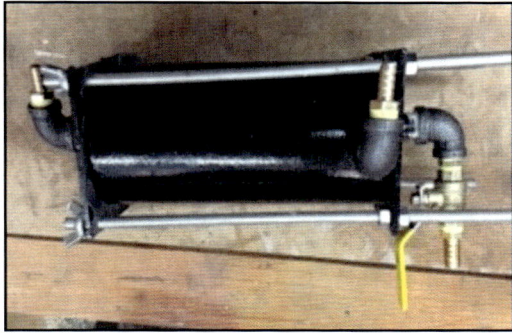

each end so I can drain it without losing vacuum. Vacuum goes
in via the side pipe, and out to the pump via the top."

Does it work? He states, "I have just started a run with green
birch, 7" thick by 14" by 15" x 2 pieces. After drawing off about
a quart of water in 8 hours, I have no pump overflow!"

He then created a drain system for the water collected. He
describes, "I attached 4' of clear nylon reinforced 3/8" I.D. tubing
to my drain pipe with a gas valve at each end. I can open the one
closest to the tank and fill the tube then close it and drain the
tube with the other end's valve. No loss of vacuum."

Jeff uses a 'normally closed' solenoid air valve in-line with the
vacuum pump. Both are on a 24-hour timer that cycles based on
the predetermined rate of leakage in the chamber. It also gets rid
of any water vapor that has accumulated. He says, "I also have a
manual valve on the vacuum line right at the vacuum outlet on
top of the kiln. When I close that I can easily drain my condenser
tank without losing much vacuum in the kiln. I normally leave

the manual vacuum line valve open when operating the kiln and let the solenoid valve do the work. I only use the manual valve when I want to drain the condenser."

If you've read this book from the beginning, you might wonder why so many of the recommendations given earlier are identical to Jeff's approach. He developed practical and affordable solutions to many of the issues presented in earlier editions, and I would be remiss if I didn't give him credit for all of them. Thanks for sharing your discoveries Jeff!

Section 5: Process for Vacuum Drying Wood

Here are the steps for drying wood using a vacuum kiln:

1. Build or buy a vacuum kiln as in Section 3 & 4
2. Source wood for your project
3. Cut wood to an even thickness
4. Batch wood with similar thickness and MC
5. Load chamber so each piece receives equal heat
6. Place temperature sensor in one piece and use this or a thermostat to control heater
7. Pull vacuum in chamber to 27 inHg or higher
8. Heat wood to 110°F (43.3°C)
9. Check MC of wood regularly
10. Keep notes

The procedure in detail

First, the kiln is loaded with wood. You can put as many items as will fit in the chamber but if it is a new setup or a new type of wood, consider drying only part of the wood for your project in case of problems. The best results come from starting with wood that has a uniform thickness throughout each piece, shares similar thickness and moisture content to the other pieces being dried, and is positioned within the kiln to reach the same temperature. (The options for applying heat are discussed in the Section 2 and my recommendations are detailed in Section 3.)

Ideally, the temperature sensor is placed centrally inside one piece of wood and this is used to control the amount of heat applied. Alternately, the temperature inside the wood could just be monitored while a separate thermostat, voltage regulator or other device controls the heater. (These approaches are further discussed in the Temperature Controller and Temperature Sensor sections in Section 3.)

If conduction heating – Draw full vacuum in the chamber while heating the wood. Drying begins when the temperature inside the wood reaches approximately 110ºF (43.3ºC) with vacuum greater than 27 inHg.

If convection heating – Modify Step 7 as follows: First draw vacuum on the chamber to around 75% of its maximum. Then seal off the chamber from the pump and begin to heat the wood. This allows some oxygen in the chamber to remain so that convection, along with a small fan, can evenly distribute the heat. When the temperature inside the wood is approximately 110ºF (43.3ºC) (which can require many hours using convection) increase the vacuum to anything greater than 27 inHg to initiate the drying process.

The moisture vapor escapes from the wood and condenses back into a liquid inside the kiln if the walls are cooler. Otherwise the vapor is pulled out of the chamber by the vacuum pump or may be collected by a moisture trap.

Until you are familiar with the drying cycle of a particular species of wood, at a specific moisture content, check the MC of the wood every 8 to 12 hours to prevent over-drying. To do this, you need to let air back into the chamber, remove the end plate and test the wood with a moisture meter. (Variables that impact the accuracy of moisture meters are discussed in Section 3.) Every time you vent the chamber, vacuum and heat is lost which halts the drying process. You will need to re-establish your constants to initiate the drying process again. Once familiar with how many hours or days it takes to dry a particular kind of wood, you can simply run a complete drying cycle without interruption.

The vacuum kiln drying process results in very consistent moisture content throughout the wood—perhaps not perfect but better than other drying methods. You may see a 1 or 2% fluctuation but this will even-out fairly quickly.

I have found it takes between half a day and three days to dry any type of wood that starts under 25% MC. The rate of drying can reach 1 to 2% per hour in ideal circumstances. Drying can happen very quickly and it is possible to go beyond your desired MC. In that case, use a box, bag or plastic wrap around the wood to slowly re-acclimate it to the ambient EMC.

It is a good idea to keep notes based on your experience, such as a record of wood species, beginning MC, drying time, number of heat/vacuum cycles, ending MC, success rate, and anything else you think will be helpful to ensure that the next drying load is a complete success. I have provided a sample Drying Notes

Template in Appendix I, which is also available as a PDF document from the Online Resources page (see Appendix V).

Common Question: Altitude

"I'm at a higher elevation than most here in Denver, CO and it seems like my pump isn't able to get as much vacuum on the chamber. What should I do?"

Air is less dense at higher elevations, so the maximum attainable vacuum level is reduced. For every 1,000 feet above sea level there is a loss of approximately one inch of inHg VAC. However, the approach for drying wood remains the same as long as you continue to achieve about 94% of the maximum attainable vacuum at your altitude. (To calculate the exact number required, see the "Vacuum Attainable at Altitude" and "Boiling Point of Liquids" tables in Appendix IV.) It is also possible your vacuum gauge reading is adversely affected by altitude. You might try a glycerin-filled vacuum gauge.

Examples for heating various loads

The photos below demonstrate some possible arrangements for using conduction heating with various types of lumber.

- Boards and thin stock
- Blocks and thick stock
- Half round stock
- Cylindrical stock
- Bowls and odd shapes

Boards and thin stock

Long thin boards can easily be stacked and heated using a variety of heat blankets and mats. It is best to layer the heaters both above and below to uniformly heat the wood. An aluminum sheet between the heater and wood can even out the heat, which helps prevent hot spots that might cause cracking, but will slow the heating process somewhat. If you only have one heat mat, it can be placed between two layers, as shown in the photo.

Blocks and thick stock

Blocks and sticks that are thicker than typical boards can be loaded and heated in the same way as boards. However, due to the insulating nature of wood that prevents the interior from achieving the same temperature as the outside, it is more important to provide heat on the both the top and bottom. Adding weight to the top, as shown in the photo, can improve surface contact that will help promote heat transfer to the load.

Half-round stock

Half-round logs and other partially rounded stock is not ideal for heating evenly due to the variation in thickness. This could result in overheating the thinner edges of the log, or a greater difference in moisture content between the edges and interior of the piece. I illustrate this type of lumber mostly because it is a common occurrence for woodturners who wish to use the natural bark edge of a log or retain the naturally rounded grain and depth for a bowl. For other uses, one would typically slab the wood to a uniform thickness, which would improve workability and also be better for heating and drying.

The shelf has been bent to support the shape of the piece being dried and provide consistent contact with the rubber heat mat. Note the addition of foam blocks to prevent the somewhat oversized heater from contacting the walls of the PVC chamber and prevent any chance of melting. An additional heat mat should be placed on top to provide more uniform heat and quicken the process.

Cylindrical stock

A silicone heat jacket used for outdoor pipes is permanently rounded and will tightly wrap itself around appropriately sized cylinders—approximately 1-1/2" to 3" diameter—perfect for the blanks I use to make boxes. The photo shows five of these being dried at once.

Flat silicone heat mats can be wrapped around cylindrical stock, but it is important not to overlap the heater onto itself because any area that is doubled-up could over-heat, ruining the heater or worse—damaging the kiln. Bungee cords placed around the heater keep it snug against the wood.

Bowls and odd shapes

Rough turned bowls and odd shapes are usually most evenly heated with convection. However, one option using conduction is to submerge the objects in an aluminum baking pan filled with aluminum or glass beads. The science industry uses aluminum oblate Lab Amor® beads which are small random bean-like shapes that can provide enough surface area to adequately transfer heat to an object. Aluminum or ceramic pie weights might be another option, though I haven't tried them yet.

The optometric industry uses a heated box filled with glass beads to reshape cellulose acetate frames. Optical supply glass beads are available in various sizes. (Again, on my list to try!) I have also been curious about the potential of using aluminum foil wrapped in and around objects and have begun some experiments that I hope to share in the next edition of this book.

More options

The above examples demonstrate various arrangements to heat lumber and you can certainly try others. Initial experiments can be done while the kiln is open to make sure everything is working as expected before sealing the chamber and applying vacuum.

Common Question: Technique 1

"Is it necessary to air–dry the wood first?"

I do think you get better results if you let the wood stabilize a bit after cutting but it's not required. I have heard that the chance of end–checking is increased with wood that starts above 25% MC. Also, resistance moisture meters aren't as accurate above 25% MC so starting in this range lets you more precisely document your drying cycles for a particular species.

"Can wood that is sealed with wax be put in the vacuum kiln?"

Wood with sealant wax on it can be dried in the vacuum kiln but the process is *much* slower. The wax will melt somewhat with higher temperatures but water vapor still cannot be released as quickly. So, unless you wish to slow the drying process, it is best to cut away or scrape off as much of the wax coating as possible prior to drying wood in the vacuum kiln.

"For convection heating, why pull a partial vacuum and then heat it? Isn't it easier to reach 110°F at normal atmosphere?"

The wood is more likely to crack when heating without vacuum and partial vacuum doesn't slow the heating process much. So, it is better to err on the side of too much vacuum rather than not enough.

"Once the wood reaches 110°F and I pump down to 27 Hg, does it matter then what the temperature is?"

Yes, keep the temperature steady at about 110°F throughout the drying process. If lower, the drying stops or, if higher, the risk of cracking is increased.

Common Question: Technique 2

"When the chamber is at 27 inHg does it continue to pull moisture out of the wood?"

The combination of temperature and vapor pressure is what initiates the drying process. But at that point the wood doesn't instantly dry; it takes a few days (depending on your beginning MC) for all the moisture in the wood to make its way out. You need to keep the kiln at the required constants throughout the duration.

"How do I get an accurate temperature of the wood?"

The surface temperature of wood usually doesn't reflect the internal temperature. Depending on the thickness there could easily be a 10°F difference or more. The process of applying heat evenly to each piece of wood is also challenging if the shape and thickness is not consistent. For convection, I recommend a heat–up cycle of four to nine hours so that the wood can fully acclimate. A temperature sensor placed inside the center of a piece of wood (rather than a thermometer in the kiln) is the best way to know what is really going on.

"After heating the wood and pulling full vacuum, does the pump need to run all the time or can I seal off the chamber and turn the pump off?"

Once you've maxed out what the pump can pull, you can turn it off but it's best to also close off the chamber since many pumps leak vacuum when they are not running. If the chamber holds vacuum you can just let it sit for the entire drying time. If vacuum drops below the required amount, you will need to pull again. In my case, I use a timer to open a solenoid valve and run the pump for thirty minutes every twelve hours.

Next step

Here are some of the results—all different kinds of wood, all with their natural colors, with no defects or drying blemishes. This is the kind of quality results you can expect.

Some of the author's woodturnings in various woods (natural colors). From top, clockwise: bloodwood, osage orange, yellowheart, padauk, lignum vitae, purpleheart, and African blackwood.

I hope this book has helped illustrate how you can build a relatively inexpensive vacuum kiln that will quickly and easily dry wood for many of your woodworking projects—reducing the time it takes from inspiration to creation, and preserving the results of your labor for generations to behold. Now it's time to take the next step— build it and use it!

If you found this book helpful, please let others know by sharing your review of it on Amazon.com or with your local woodworking group. I also welcome your thoughts on how it might be enhanced along with any specific questions you'd like answered so that I may improve future editions of the book.

Common Comments

"I am starting at 31% moisture with 3x3 cylinders that are 6 inches long. Wow– What a process! One piece is at 6.8% when I checked it this evening. The others are 12–14%. I have no warping or cracks. Thanks so much for sharing this process and writing the book."
—*Sharon*

"I live in the country in North Central Texas. I purchased your book a little over a year ago. My interest in a quick way to cure lumber made me start surfing the web. Your book filled the bill. I have made a kiln a little larger than yours, of course being from Texas. It is 10 feet long, 24" in diameter, with 1/2" steel walls. A little over a year ago, I started trying to make the thing work. Over a year, many dollars, and a lot of trial and error, and a lot of help from your book, it is perfected. The key to it is a very large Ingersoll Rand Vacuum Pump, a very controllable heating system and I was in business. Can cure most woods on my place in about four days. Just wanted you to know that your book has been a tremendous help in this endeavor. Thanks!"
—*Steve*

"I just wanted to give you an update on my kiln: Initially I was unable to remove moisture from the wood even at a very high vacuum. I'm now heating the kiln load to 115°F and the results are amazing! It took material that was 22%+ MC down to 9–13% (depending on the piece) in just 36 hours."
—*Brian*

Appendix I – Drying Template

Until you are familiar with the drying cycle of a particular species of wood, at a specific moisture content, check the MC of the wood frequently to prevent over-drying. This may be once every half a day or once every couple of days depending on your setup and the beginning MC of the wood you are drying.

It's a good idea to keep notes based on your experience, such as a record of wood species, beginning MC, drying time, number of heat/vacuum cycles, ending MC, success rate, and anything else you think will be helpful to ensure that the next drying load will be a complete success.

Below is an example followed by a couple blank templates you can use. You can also download a PDF version of the template from the Online Resources page (see Appendix V).

Vacuum Kiln Drying Notes

Date: July 4, 2017

Number of Items: 12

Dimensions:

4"dia bowls

Species:

cocobolo, blackwood, purpleheart, osage

Drying cycle:

Day	Beginning	Hours	Cycles	Ending MC
1	16%	24	30m on / 11h 30m off	12%
2	12%	24	30m on / 11h 30m off	7%
3				
4				
5				

Results:

Seems blackwood is measuring a bit drier than others. Might be density of wood / moisture meter issue. No checking noted upon removal. Note: 80°F temperature outside during drying cycle.

Vacuum Kiln Drying Notes

Date:

Number of Items:

Dimensions:

Species:

Drying cycle:

Day	Beginning	Hours	Cycles	Ending MC
1				
2				
3				
4				
5				

Results:

Vacuum Kiln Drying Notes

Date:

Number of Items:

Dimensions:

Species:

Drying cycle:

Day	Beginning	Hours	Cycles	Ending MC
1				
2				
3				
4				
5				

Results:

Appendix II – Wiring Diagrams for the ITC-1000-F Temperature Controller

The ITC-1000-F temperature controller is sold with a variety of rebranding. The "F" indicates it can display in Fahrenheit in addition to Celsius. The wiring diagram included with my unit was incorrect so I thought it would be useful to provide a correct diagram along with a few possible configurations. (Double check your unit to be sure it is laid out the same way before wiring.)

- AC power cord for direct plug-in
- Outlet for multiple plugs (heating only)
- Split outlet for heating with optional cooling

The simplest method of wiring the temperature controller is to connect the included temperature sensor to the appropriate terminals and then wire the male end of an AC power cord directly to the unit's power and heating control terminals.

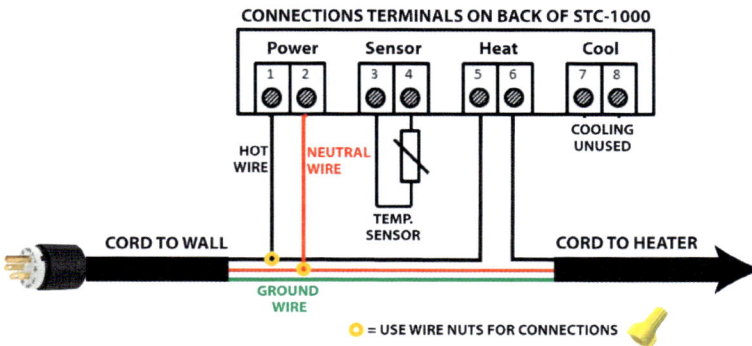

CONNECTIONS TERMINALS ON BACK OF STC-1000

To use an outlet, such as a GFCI, the connections should be done like this:

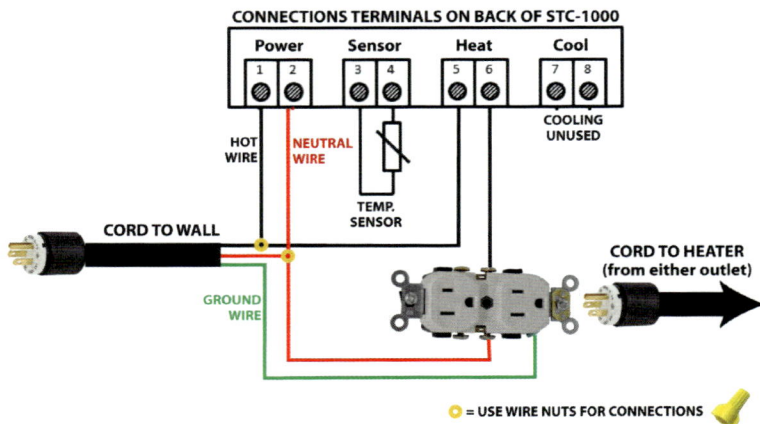

Another option is to split the outlet (GFCI outlets can't be split so you'll have to use a standard one) so that both the heating and cooling aspects of the temperature controller can be utilized. In this configuration, the temperature setting determines the point at which the controller will power one side of the outlet (connected to a heater to heat the wood) and then a "difference set value" setting determines the point at which the controller will power the other side of the outlet (connected to a fan or air-conditioner to cool the exterior chamber walls).

The temperature controller and an outlet will fit in a deep two-gang electrical box.

In this case, the wiring should be completed as in the following diagram:

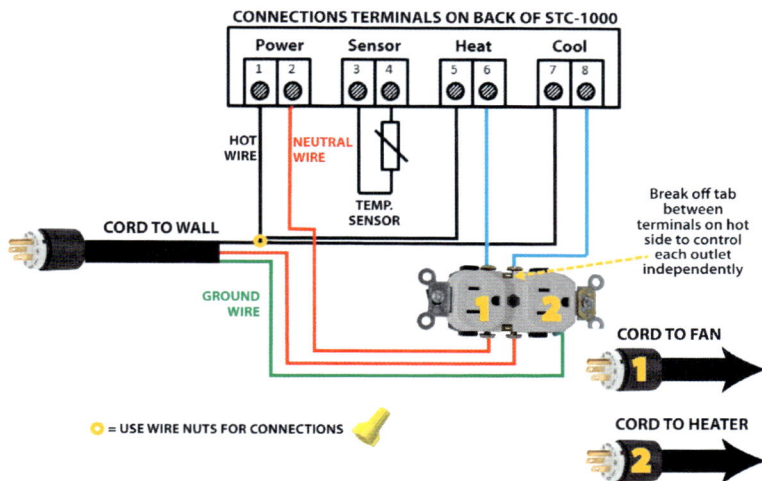

An important note for the above wiring is that you MUST break the tab on the hot side (the wires that connect to terminal 6 & 8). Keep the other tab on the neutral side intact.

While this arrangement does make the most of the controller's capability, it has limited functionally because it is more useful to be able to control the cooling both independently and simultaneous along with the heating. (That arrangement is possible with an additional temperature controller.)

Example Settings

Here are some ITC-1000F (Fahrenheit) example settings to demonstrate how the previous wiring arrangement would function:

Setting	Screen	Value
Temperature Set	TS	120
Difference Set	DS	9
Compressor Delay	PT	0
Temperature Calibration	CA	0
ºF or ºC Settings	CF	F

Using the above settings, the outlet wired to the heat control will be powered until the temperature sensor reaches 120ºF. The outlet wired to the cooling control will be powered if and when the temperature sensor reaches 129ºF and will continue until the temperature has fallen to 119ºF. The heat control outlet will not be powered again until the temperature sensor continues to fall to 110ºF at which point it will power the heat control outlet until 120ºF is again reached, and the cycle will continue indefinitely.

Appendix III – Modifications for Stabilizing Wood

After drying wood, it is possible to also use the vacuum kiln setup detailed in this book to stabilize it. This is the process of adding resin, which creates a very hard material allowing the use of wood or other organic material that would otherwise be too soft. In addition, dye can be added to color the material creating interesting and unusual possibilities.

Examples of dyed and stabilized sycamore and maple burl. Photo courtesy of BurlSource.

To do this, you will need to be able to see what is going on inside the chamber. The chamber is often placed vertically on its end and an acrylic or polycarbonate end plate is utilized. (Approximate minimum thickness to use: ¾" for a 12" cylinder, 1.5" for an 18" cylinder and 3" for a 24" diameter.)

You might add a second inlet valve connected to a clear flexible tube to feed the liquid resin to a container big enough to submerge the material. Alternately you could initially fill the container with resin and then seal the chamber and start the vacuum pump.

In brief, air from the wood is pulled out and replaced by the resin. Over time the material will completely absorb the resin after which it is removed and sealed for the curing process.

The process outlined here is obviously just a concise introduction. Visit the Online Resources page (see Appendix V) for recommended links that provide further details.

Appendix IV – Reference Charts

Equilibrium moisture content (EMC)

The EMC of wood changes quite a lot with the ambient relative humidity and to a lesser degree with temperature. Wood should be dried to a final moisture content based on the environment where it will be used. The dashed box area indicates the typical MC range for a climate-controlled indoor environment.

Equilibrium Moisture Content

				Temperature			
	30° F	40° F	50° F	60° F	70° F	80° F	90° F
20%	4.6	4.6	4.6	4.6	4.5	4.4	4.3
25%	5.5	5.5	5.5	5.4	5.4	5.3	5.1
30%	6.3	6.3	6.3	6.2	6.2	6.1	5.9
35%	7.1	7.1	7.1	7.0	6.9	6.8	6.7
40%	7.9	7.9	7.9	7.8	7.7	7.6	7.4
45%	8.7	8.7	8.7	8.6	8.5	8.3	8.1
50%	9.5	9.5	9.5	9.4	9.2	9.1	8.9
55%	10.4	10.4	10.3	10.2	10.1	9.9	9.7
60%	11.3	11.3	11.2	11.1	11.0	10.8	10.5
65%	12.4	12.3	12.3	12.1	12.0	11.7	11.5
70%	13.5	13.5	13.4	13.3	13.1	12.9	12.6
75%	14.9	14.9	14.8	14.6	14.4	14.2	13.9
80%	16.5	16.5	16.4	16.2	16.0	15.7	15.4
85%	18.5	18.5	18.4	18.2	17.9	17.7	17.3
90%	21.0	21.0	20.9	20.7	20.5	20.2	19.8
95%	24.3	24.3	24.3	24.1	23.9	23.6	23.3

Relative Humidity (vertical axis label)

Boiling point of water

The table below provides the temperature at which vapor pressure created by the vacuum pump is sufficient to begin transforming "unbound" water (not in wood cells) to vapor. The dashed box area indicates the general range for vacuum kiln drying.

Inches of Hg VAC	Boiling Point at Sea Level	
	F°	C°
0.00	212	100
4.92	205	96.11
9.23	194	90
15.94	176	80
20.72	158	70
24.04	140	60
26.28	122	50
27.75	104	40
28.67	86	30
28.92	80	26.67
29.02	76	24.44
29.12	72	22.22
29.22	69	20.56
29.32	64	17.78
29.42	59	15
29.52	53	11.67
29.62	45	7.22
29.74	32	0
29.82	21	-6.11
29.87	6	-14.44
29.91	-24	-31.11
29.915	-35	-37.22

Below is a graph of the table from the previous page. This visual representation makes clear the requirement for strong vacuum that enables relatively low temperatures to produce the evaporation of water. The dashed box area indicates the general range for vacuum kiln drying.

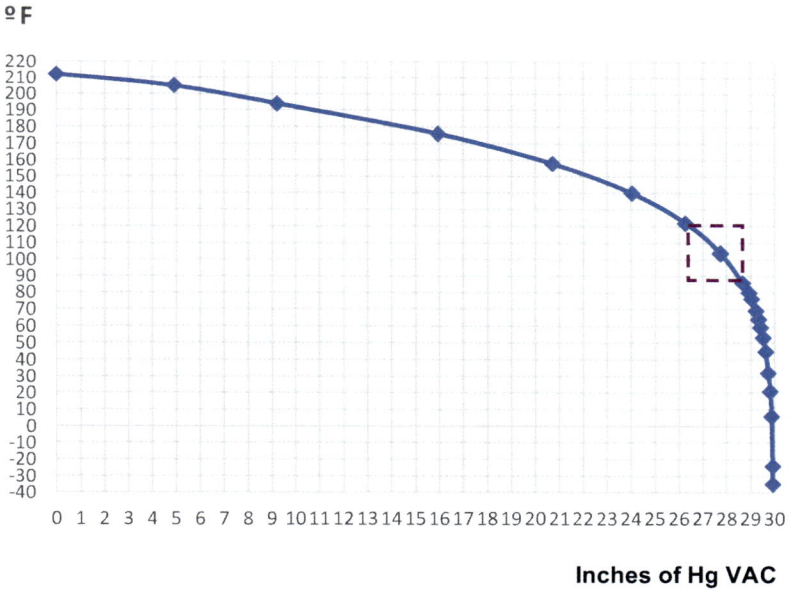

Vacuum attainable at altitude

The maximum attainable vacuum at higher altitude is reduced since air is less dense. For every 1,000 feet above sea level, there is a loss of approximately one inch of Hg VAC.

Altitude Above Sea Level (feet)	Altitude Above Sea Level (meters)	Maximum Attainable Vacuum (inches Hg VAC)	Maximum Attainable Vacuum Altitude (percent)
0	0	29.9	99.9
1000	305	28.9	96.6
2000	610	27.8	92.9
3000	914	26.8	89.6
4000	1219	25.8	86.2
5000	1524	24.9	83.2
6000	1829	24.0	80.2
7000	2134	23.1	77.2
8000	2438	22.2	74.1
9000	2743	21.4	71.4
10,000	3048	20.6	68.7

The method for drying wood at higher elevations remains the same as long as you continue to achieve about 94% of the maximum attainable vacuum at your altitude. You can calculate this as follows:

1. Determine the percent of maximum attainable vacuum for your altitude using the table above (dashed box area).
2. Multiply that percentage by the vacuum required for the temperature of the wood being dried (using the Boiling Point of Water table on the preceding page).
3. Multiply that result by .94 for your target inHg VAC.

Comparison of pressure measurements

As you research vacuum pumps and related topics you may find these comparison pressure measurements to be helpful.

mm Hg Torr	Inches Hg VAC	% VAC	mbar	Inches Hg Abs	Micron
760	0	0	1013	29.99	760,000
500	10.3	34	667	19.70	500,000
200	22.1	74	267	7.85	200,000
100	26.0	87	133.3	3.94	100,000
90	26.5	88	120	3.54	90,000
80	26.8	89.5	107	3.15	80,000
70	27.2	90.8	93	2.76	70,000
60	27.6	92.1	80	2.36	60,000
50	28.0	93.5	67	1.97	50,000
40	28.4	94.8	53	1.57	40,000
30	28.8	96.1	40	1.18	30,000
20	29.2	97.4	27	0.78	20,000
10	29.6	98.7	13.3	0.39	10,000
5	29.7	99.0	6.6	0.03	5,000
1	29.95	99.9	1.33	0.039	1,000
1×10^{-1}	29.99	99.99	1.3×10^{-1}	0.009	100
1×10^{-2}			1.3×10^{-2}		10
1×10^{-3}			1.3×10^{-3}		1
1×10^{-4}			1.3×10^{-4}		1×10^{-1}

Conversion factors

As you research vacuum pumps and related topics you may find these conversion factors to be helpful.

mm Hg Torr	Inches Hg VAC	% VAC
inches	to mm	x 25.4
ft^3	to liters	x 28.32
inches^3	to cm^3	x 15.387
m^3	to ft^3	x 35.31
ft^3	to m^3	x 0.02832
gallon	to inches^3	x 231
gallon	to liters	x 3.87
gallon	to lb h$_2$O (at 60°F)	x 8.338
m^3/hr	to ft^3/min	x 0.589
liters/min	to ft^3/min	x 0.0353
Torr	to mbar	x 1.33
Torr	to PSI	x 0.0193
Mbar	to Torr	x 0.75
Torr	to PASCAL	x 133.32
inches inHg VAC	to PSI	x 0.491
Torr	to Micron	x 1.000

Appendix V – Online Resources

Links to articles related to wood drying and vacuum technology, downloads to useful templates and reference charts, as well as useful websites for parts and supplies can be found online at www.vacuumkilndrying.com/resources.html

Learn more about
- Wood drying
- Vacuum technology
- PVC pipe

Download files
- Vacuum kiln drying template
- Equilibrium moisture content
- Boiling point of water
- Vacuum attainable at altitude
- Comparison of pressure measurements
- Conversion factors

Find related suppliers
- General vacuum supply companies (for chambers, pumps, water traps and related hardware)
- Thermometer, thermistor and thermostat suppliers
- Heating element suppliers
- Commercial wood vacuum drying kilns
- Other related suppliers

Link to project parts, pricing, and reviews
- Kiln hardware
- Heating
- Sealants
- Moisture traps
- Moisture meters & other gauges
- Other items

About the Author

Joshua Salesin has produced a variety of turned, carved and decorative wood vessels for many years. A particular focus of his work is the uncommon craft of ornamental turning.

His interest in vacuum kiln drying originated from a desire to create fine hand-cut threaded boxes, which require tolerances that leave little room for wood movement.

Salesin lives and works in northern California and can be reached via his website at www.joshuasalesin.com.

Made in the USA
Las Vegas, NV
23 December 2020